Basic Economic Law of
Monopoly Capitalism
Transition to
Imperialism

Ostrovityanov K.V. Shepilov D.T. Leontiev L.A.
Laptev I.D. Kuzminov I.I. Gatovsky L.M

Svitlana M, Erdogan A

From The Political Economy Text Book

Translated From Russian; S.M

Edited by; E.A

State publishing house of political literature. Moscow. 1954

Sole purpose is to share what we have studied for our education with the other interested parties.

Contents

Introduction

The definition of "imperialism" used in order to determine if a country is imperialist or not generally is limited to its **economic aspect**, disregarding the "political" aspect. Lenin in his forward to Imperialism stated that "pamphlet was written with an eye to the tsarist censorship. Hence," he said, "I was not only forced to **confine myself strictly to an exclusively theoretical, specifically economic analysis of facts,** but to formulate the **few necessary** observations **on politics** with extreme caution... I trust that this pamphlet will help the reader to understand the fundamental **economic question,** that of the **economic essence of imperialism."** (1)

Lenin was pointing this out by saying; **"imperialism can and must be defined differently** if we bear in mind not only the basic, **purely economic** concepts—to which **the above definition is limited.."** (1)

It was Lenin himself saying that his "imperialism" and definition is **limited to economic aspect of it.** In reference to Imperialism, and importance of this question Lenin points out that;

> "The problem of imperialism is not only a **most essential** one, but, we may say it is the most essential problem in that realm of economic science which examines the changing forms of capitalism in recent times. Everyone interested not only in economics but in any sphere of present-day social life must acquaint himself with the facts relating to this problem, as presented by the author in such detail on the basis of the latest available data. Needless to say that **there can be**

no concrete historical analysis of war, if that analysis does not have for its basis a full understanding of the nature of imperialism, **both from its economic and political aspects.** Without this, it is impossible to approach an understanding of the economic and diplomatic situation of the last decades, and without such an understanding, **it is ridiculous even to speak of forming a correct view on the war."** (2)

In his critique of Kautsky he summarized the policy in one word- use of force.

""Imperialism is a striving for annexations... It is correct, but very incomplete, for **politically,** imperialism is, in general, a **striving towards violence and reaction.**".. The essence of the matter is that Kautsky **detaches the politics of imperialism from its economics...Finance capital and the trusts do not diminish but increase the differences in the rate of growth of the various parts of the world economy.** Once the relation of forces is changed, what other solution of the contradictions can be found **under capitalism than that of force?"** *(1)*

Bukharin in his book which the introduction is written by Lenin, deals with the definitions of imperialism. He states;

The second very widespread "theory" of imperialism defines it as the **policy of conquest in general**... Simple as this theory may be, it is absolutely untrue. **It is untrue** because it "explains" everything, i.e., **it explains absolutely nothing.**

Every policy of the ruling classes ("pure" policy, military policy, economic policy) **has a perfectly definite functional significance... War serves** to reproduce definite relations of production. **War of conquest** serves to reproduce those relations on a wider scale. Simply to **define war,** however, **as conquest is entirely insufficient,** for the simple reason that in doing so we **fail to indicate the main thing, namely,** what production relations are **strengthened** or **extended by the war,** what basis is widened **by a given "policy of conquest...** Bourgeois science does not see and does not wish to see this. It **does not understand** that a basis for the classification of **various "policies" must exist in the social economy out of which the "policies" arise. "** (3)

Defining imperialism as a **"specific historic category"** he points out the mistakes of approach which coincidently mistakes of our days too. He states that Imperialism; "upholds the **structure of finance capital**; it subjugates the world to the **domination of finance capital;** in place of the old capitalist, production relations, it puts the **production relations of finance capital.** Just as finance capitalism (which **must not be confused with money capital,** for finance capital is characterized by being simultaneously **banking and industrial capital)** is an historically limited epoch, confined only to the last few decades, so imperialism, as the policy of finance capital, is a specific historic category."

"**war is** a continuation of politics by other **means**... Politics itself, however, is **an active "continuation."** (3)

An abstract repetition of "war is a continuation of politics by other means", as if it explains everything is a common ready-made solution used to all questions of wars, however, **without actually studying** the given "politics" itself under that given concrete conditions.

"Capitalist society" says Bukharin, "is **unthinkable without armaments**, as it is **unthinkable without wars.** And just as it is true that not low prices cause competition but, on the contrary, competition causes low prices, it is equally true that **not the existence of arms is the prime cause** and the moving force in wars (although **wars are obviously impossible without arms**) but, on the contrary, the **inevitableness of economic conflicts conditions the existence of arms**. This is why in our times, when economic conflicts have reached an unusual degree of intensity, we are witnessing a **mad orgy of armaments.** Thus **the rule of finance capital implies both imperialism and militarism.** In this sense militarism is **no less a typical** historic phenomenon than finance capital itself... even where there are **relatively equal** economic structures, but the **military powers** of the state capitalist trusts differ considerably." (3)

Thus, Imperialism and war are inseparable twins. That is why the issue of "imperialism" and attitude to it cannot be studied independently from its political aspect- that is *(militarization of industry and)* war- in each given concrete condition and situation. Lenin was saying that **"Abstract theoretical reasoning** may lead to the conclusion at which Kautsky has arrived .. by abandoning Marxism. It goes without saying that there can be no concrete historical assessment of war, unless it is based on a thorough **analysis of the nature of imperialism,** both in its economic and political aspects." (1) Connecting the two Lenin points out that "The character of a war and its success **depend chiefly upon** the internal regime of the country

7

that goes to war, that **war is a reflection of the internal policy** conducted by the given country before the war. " (4)

"If they are both sides of the same coin" some will say, " then **our attitude to a "war" will not be different than our attitude to "imperialism"**. However, Lenin clearly points out that "depending on historical conditions, the relationship of classes and similar data, **the attitude towards war must be different at different times**. " *(5)* That, dialectically means, the attitude to "imperialism" will be different at different times. There will be times, conditions, and situations where there is no **"interests of proletariat in general"** but only the **"interests of proletariat" in particular.** There will be times, conditions, and situations where, because of the existence of a "general interests of proletariat", the interests of particular will be subordinated to the interests of the general. In a **constantly changing world** the conditions and situations will change, so the attitude to each will have to be changed.   That is why, **"it is not surprising"** says Lenin, " that Marx and the Marxists confined themselves to determining which bourgeoisie's victory would be more harmless to (or more favourable to) the world proletariat, **at a time when one could not speak** of a general proletarian movement against the governments and the bourgeoisie of all the belligerent countries." *(6)*

Lenin in his critique of Potresoy clarifies the old and new epochs and their class context in regard to Marx attitude to the wars and the question of the "the success of which bourgeoisie is more desirable" says; " Potresov has failed to notice that **Marx was working on the problem at a time when there existed** indubitably progressive bourgeois movements, which moreover did not merely exist, but were in the forefront of the historical process in the leading states of Europe. **Today, it would be ridiculous** even to imagine a progressive bourgeoisie, a progressive bourgeois movement, in, for instance, such key members of the "Concert" of Europe, as Britain and Germany." (*12*)

Marx's view and approach to the Tsarist regime as the **main focus of reaction** and counterrevolution in the world, and had to be fought harder than any other **was not his general political line on war and peace** but related to the **that given concrete situation and conditions.**

"**In the first epoch**," says Lenin, " the objective and historical task was to ascertain how, in its struggle against the chief representatives of a dying feudalism, the progressive bourgeoisie should "utilize" international conflicts so as to bring the greatest possible advantage to the entire democratic bourgeoisie of the world... the possession of colonies and the expansion of colonial possessions... **The second epoch** is...the deep contradictions in modern democracy... the cities were attracting ever more inhabitants, and living conditions in the large cities of the whole world were being levelled out; capital was becoming internationalized, and at the big factories townsmen and country-folk, both native and alien, were intermingling. The class contradictions were growing ever more acute... **in the third epoch**, no feudal fortresses of all-European significance remain... it is the task of present-day democracy to "utilize" conflicts, but this international utilization must be directed, **not against individual national finance capital,** but **against international finance capital.**" (*13*)

Aside from being "the bygone period of bourgeois democratic revolutions against feudalism", during the first world war **Lenin's attitude was not the same before the revolution and after the revolution**. The attitude derived from **not by generalized theories** but from the interests of proletariat and of their struggle. First period, in the case of Russia, **consideration** was the **interests of revolutionary struggle**, second was **the interests of revolution itself.**

Marxist dialectical method **forbids the employment of "ready-made schemes" and abstract formulas,** The dialectical method demands, first, that we should consider things, not each by itself, but always in their interconnection with other things. That means **even in the same epoch,** the same war attitude may change as **the character of war may change** with the possible changes in the belligerent countries.

While criticizing Rosa Lenin was saying; "**we remain dialecticians** and we **combat sophistry** not by denying the possibility of all transformations in general, but by analysing the given phenomenon in its concrete setting and development... This "epoch" has made the policies of the present great powers thoroughly imperialist... Objectively, the feudal and dynastic wars were **then** opposed by revolutionary democratic wars, by wars for national liberation. This was the content of the **historical tasks of that epoch.** At the **present time,** the objective situation in the biggest advanced states of Europe **is different**...From the standpoint of progress, from the standpoint of the progressive class, the **imperialist bourgeois war, the war of highly developed capitalism,** can, objectively, be opposed **only with a war against the bourgeoisie,** i.e., **primarily civil war** for power between the proletariat and the bourgeoisie.. Marxist **dialectics call** for a **concrete analysis** of each specific historical situation... **Civil war** against the bourgeoisie is also **a form of class struggle..**" *(7)*

Based on his analysis of concrete situation in that given time and conditions, the "Revolutionary **Defeatism**" stand of Lenin worked. "**Civil war became a fact**" said Lenin on Extraordinary Seventh Congress. " The transformation of the imperialist war into civil war, which we had predicted at the beginning of the revolution, and even at the beginning of the war... circumstances in which we found ourselves in October..." (*8)*

The "defeatist" stand transformed in to **"Defencist"** stand. "Yes, we are now defencists" said Lenin. "We have been **defencists since October** 25, 1917; we have won the right to defend our native land... it is a policy of preparation for defense of our country, a steadfast policy, not allowing a single step to be taken that would aid the **extremist parties of the imperialist powers** in the East and West." *(9)* Following, Lenin states that this **"right"** to **"defend"** from the **"defeatist"** stand **"is not achieved by** issuing declarations, but only by overthrowing the bourgeoisie in one's own country. In that matter, he states; " it **would be absurd** to **concoct a recipe,** or **general rule** that would serve in all cases. One must **have the brains to analyze** the situation in each separate case." (10)

Either defeatist, or defencist or (active) neutral, stands of Marxist Leninists derive from **the fundamental principle** of having the interests of proletariat and of its struggle **in mind** when we make an evaluation for the policy and stand. It is never a narrowminded, mechanical question of which side or more like which bourgeois will be beneficial to us, **it is the**

question of where the interests of proletariat lie – not based on **abstract general theories** but- based on concrete conditions.

This principle was what Stalin followed and applied during the second world war. In a very similar way to First World War, he made agreement with aggressive (Lenin calls extremist) Imperialist Germany to prepare for the 2nd imperialist World War. He reached to **non-aggressive imperialists** for an alliance for peace. He states;

> "A distinguishing feature of the new crisis is that it differs in many respects from the preceding one, and, moreover, differs for the worse and not for the better. …the present crisis has broken out **not in time of peace,** but at a time when a second imperialist war has already begun.. when all the other big capitalist powers are beginning to reorganize themselves **on a war footing**."
>
> "…as distinct from the preceding crisis, the present crisis is not a general one, but as yet involves chiefly the economically powerful countries which have not yet placed themselves on a war economy basis. As regards the **aggressive countries**, such as Japan, Germany, and Italy, who have already reorganized their economy on a war footing, they, because of the intense development of their war industry, are not yet experiencing a crisis of overproduction, although they are approaching it. This means that by the time the economically powerful, **non-aggressive countries** begin to emerge from the phase of crisis the aggressive countries, having exhausted their reserves of gold and raw material in the course of the war fever, are bound to enter a phase of very severe crisis.

... It is no longer a question of competition in the markets, of a commercial war, of dumping. These methods of struggle have long been recognized as inadequate. **It is now a question of a new redivision of the world,** of spheres of influence and colonies, by military action...the **bloc of three aggressive states** came to be formed. A new redivision of the world by means of war became imminent.

After the first imperialist war the victor states, primarily Britain, France, and the United States, set up a new regime in the relations between countries, the post-war peace regime. .. However, three a**ggressive states**, Japan tore up the Nine-Power Pact, and Germany and Italy the Versailles Treaty, and the **new imperialist war launched by them,** upset the entire system of this post-war peace regime... The new imperialist war became a fact." (11)

The determination of the **type of war was not different** – it was an "imperialist war," but with distinctions from the previous imperialist war. Stalin evaluated the character of this distinction with the questions;

To what are we to attribute this one-sided and strange character of the new imperialist war?

How is it that the **non-aggressive countries,** which possess such vast opportunities, have so easily and without resistance abandoned their positions and their obligations **to please the aggressors**?

Is it to be attributed to the weakness of the non-aggressive states? Of course not! Combined, the non-aggressive, democratic states are unquestionably stronger than the fascist states, both economically and militarily.

To what then are we to attribute the **systematic concessions made by these states to the aggressors**? (11)

Stalin was clearly **making a distinction** between the *(extremist)* **aggressive** imperialists and **non-aggressive** imperialists. He explained;

> "The chief reason is that the majority of the non-aggressive countries, particularly Britain and France, have rejected the policy of collective security, the policy of collective resistance to aggressors, and have taken up a position of non-intervention, a position of "neutrality." (11)

In reference to "neutrality," "non-intervention" which is so widely used as a ready-made formulas, Stalin's explanation was enlightening;

> Formally speaking, the **policy of non-intervention** might be defined as follows:
> "Let each country defend itself a**gainst the aggressors** as it likes and **as best it can.** That is not our affair We shall trade both with the aggressors and with their victims."
> But actually speaking, **the policy of non-intervention means conniving at aggression,** giving free rein to war, and, consequently, **transforming the war into a world war.** The policy of non-intervention **reveals an eagerness, a desire,** not to hinder the aggressors in their nefarious work. (11)

Stalin did not have the illusion that the non-aggressive imperialists will not change its character. His policy was the **policy of "utilizing" the contradictions** between the imperialist powers for the best **interests of the proletariat in particular and in general.** Existing conditions and situations required for the duration the task to be "utilizing" the conflict, **not against all international finance capital** but against individual national finance capital, whereas before the October Revolution, **during the first world war , it was the other way around.**

Stalin clearly stated that " the Second World War began not as a war with the U.S.S.R., but as a war between capitalist countries...the inevitability of wars between capitalist countries remains in force... To eliminate the inevitability of war, it is necessary to abolish imperialism. (14)

In brief, **"imperialism" by its general and economic "definition"** is **not decisive** in every situation and condition to determine the specific stand to be taken against.

Widely quoted and repeated definition of imperialism by Lenin is largely limited to its economic aspects of it. Especially the fifth condition "already completed division of the world", refers to the "victories imperialists" for an epoch that is completed. One cannot use that for China, for example, because China was a colony at that time. It is a bygone period that defines the victorious of the imperialists of that given era. As Stalin noted; "The redistribution of the world and spheres of influence, carried out as a result of the last imperialist war, has already managed **to become "obsolete"**. Some new countries have come forward.. A furious struggle is going on for sales markets, for markets for the export of capital, for sea and land roads to these markets, for a new redivision of the world... the growth of all these contradictions means the growth of the crisis of world capitalism, despite the fact of stabilization, a crisis incomparably deeper than the crisis before the last imperialist war... It is not surprising that imperialism is preparing for a new war, seeing in it the only way to resolve this crisis." (16)

Due to the law of uneven economic development **new "imperialist"** countries emerge a**gainst the old**-victorious ones. "The law of uneven development in the period of imperialism" says Stalin, " means the spasmodic development of some countries in relation to others, the rapid ousting of some countries from the world market by others, the **periodic redistribution of the already divided world** in the order of military clashes and military catastrophes... the fact that the **world has already been divided among imperialist groups,** there are no more "free", unoccupied territories in the world, and in order to occupy new markets and sources of raw materials, in order to expand, one must take from others this territory by force... the unprecedented development of technology.. made it easier for some countries to leap ahead of others, for the more powerful countries to be ousted by less powerful but rapidly developing countries. the old distribution of spheres of influence between individual imperialist groups each time comes into conflict with the new alignment of forces on the world market... The world imperialist war was the first attempt to redistribute an already divided world. Needless to say, the **first attempt at redistribution must be followed by a second attempt**, for which preparatory work is already underway in the imperialist camp." (15)

Old imperialist countries already have their **"military industry"** and ready for a new war militarily. New ones are in the process of building their military industry and getting ready for a new war. That's why they choose the **"appeasement policy"** against the "old" as much as possible to do so. Here comes the **question of "policy"** that is repeated abstractly without answering the question of; what is the **actual** *(domestic and foreign)* policy that is being followed by each belligerent country **before the war**.?

Without studying this "policy" concretely, repeating the statement that "war is a continuation of policy in different form", **"explains absolutely nothing."**

Finishing up with Stalin's words;

> Many people think that **imperialist pacifism is an instrument of peace.** This is fundamentally wrong. Imperialist **pacifism is an instrument for preparing for war** and for covering up this preparation with Pharisaic phrases about peace. Without such pacifism...the preparation of wars under present conditions is impossible.
>
> There are **naive people** who think that if there is imperialist pacifism, **then there will be no war.** This is completely false. On the contrary, whoever wants to get the truth must reverse this situation and say: since imperialist pacifism ...flourishes, **there will certainly be new imperialist wars and interventions.**

Svitlana M, Erdogan A

Transition to imperialism.

Pre-monopoly capitalism with the dominance of free competition reached its highest point of development by the 1960s and 1970s. During the last third of the 19th century, the transition from pre-monopoly capitalism to monopoly capitalism took place. In the late 19th and early 20th centuries, monopoly capitalism finally took shape.

Monopoly capitalism, or imperialism, is the highest and last stage of capitalism, the main distinguishing feature of which is the replacement of free competition by the rule of monopolies. The transition from pre-monopoly capitalism to monopoly capitalism - imperialism - was prepared by the entire process of development of the productive forces and production relations of bourgeois society.

The last third of the 19th century was marked by major technical shifts, the growth of industry and its concentration. In metallurgy, new methods of steel smelting (Bessemer, Tomas, open-hearth) have been widely used. The rapid spread of new types of engines - dynamo, internal combustion engine, steam turbine, electric motor - accelerated the development of industry and transport. Advances in science and technology opened up the possibility of producing electrical energy on a mass scale at thermal and then at large hydroelectric power stations. The use of electrical energy led to the creation of a number of new branches of the chemical industry, metallurgy of non-ferrous and light metals. The use of chemical methods in many industries has expanded.

As early as the middle of the 19th century, light industry occupied a predominant place in the industry of the capitalist countries. Numerous enterprises of relatively small size belonged to individual owners; the proportion of joint-stock companies was relatively small. The economic crisis of 1873 brought many such enterprises to ruin and gave a strong impetus to the concentration and centralization of capital. The predominant role in the industry of the main capitalist countries began to be played by heavy industry, primarily metallurgy and machine building, as well as mining, the development of which required enormous capital. The widespread use of joint-stock companies further strengthened the centralization of capital.

The volume of world industrial output tripled between 1870 and 1900. World steel production increased from 0.5 million tons in 1870 to 28 million tons in 1900, and world pig iron production from 12.2 million tons to 40.7 million tons. The development of energy, metallurgy and chemistry led to an increase in world coal production (from 218 million tons in 1870 to 769 million tons in 1900) and oil (from 0.8 million tons to 20 million tons). The growth of industrial production was closely linked with the development of rail transport. In 1835, 10 years after the construction of the first railway, there were 2.4 thousand kilometers of railway tracks all over the world, in 1870 - over 200 thousand, and in 1900 - 790 thousand kilometers. Sea routes began to be served by large ships driven by steam engines and internal combustion engines.

During the 19th century, the capitalist mode of production spread rapidly throughout the globe. Back in the early 70s of the last century, the oldest bourgeois country - England -

produced more fabrics, smelted more iron, mined more coal than the United States of America, Germany, France, Italy, Russia, and Japan combined. England held the primacy in world industrial production and an undivided monopoly on the world market. By the end of the 19th century, the situation had changed dramatically. The young capitalist countries have grown their own large-scale industry. In terms of industrial production, the United States of America ranked first in the world, and Germany ranked first in Europe. Despite the obstacles created by the thoroughly rotten tsarist regime, Russia quickly followed the path of industrial development.

As the transition to imperialism proceeded, the contradictions between the productive forces and the production relations of capitalism began to take on ever sharper forms. The subordination of production to the predatory goals of the capitalists' pursuit of the highest profit has created numerous obstacles to the development of productive forces and technical progress. Economic crises of overproduction began to recur more frequently, their destructive power increased, and the army of the unemployed grew. Along with the growth of poverty and deprivation of the working masses of town and countryside, there was an unprecedented increase in wealth concentrated in the hands of a handful of exploiters. The aggravation of irreconcilable class contradictions between the bourgeoisie and the proletariat led to the intensification of the economic and political struggle of the working class.

During the period of transition to imperialism, the major capitalist powers of Europe and America seized vast colonial possessions by force and deceit. A small handful of capitalistically developed countries have turned the majority of the world's population into colonial slaves who hate their oppressors and fight against them. Colonial conquests have greatly expanded the field of capitalist exploitation; the degree of exploitation of the working masses steadily increased. The extreme aggravation of the contradictions of capitalism has found expression in the devastating imperialist wars that claim many human lives and destroy enormous material values.

The historical merit of the Marxist study of imperialism as the highest and at the same time the last stage in the development of capitalism, as the eve of the socialist revolution of the proletariat, belongs to VI Lenin. In his classic work Imperialism, the Highest Stage of Capitalism and in a number of other works written mainly during the First World War, Lenin summed up the development of world capitalism in the half century since the publication of Marx's Capital. Relying on the laws of the emergence, development and decline of capitalism discovered by Marx and Engels, Lenin gave an exhaustive scientific analysis of the economic and political essence of imperialism, its laws, and insoluble contradictions.

According to Lenin's classical definition, the main economic features of imperialism are: "1) the concentration of production and capital, which has reached such a high stage of development that it has created monopolies that play a decisive role in economic life; 2) the merging of banking capital with industrial capital and the creation, on the basis of this "financial capital", of a financial oligarchy; 3) the export of capital, in contrast to the export of goods, is of particular importance; 4) international monopoly unions of capitalists are formed, dividing the world, and 5) the territorial division of the land by the major capitalist powers is completed" [1] .

Concentration of production and monopoly. Monopolies and competition.

In the pre-monopoly period, under the rule of free competition, the operation of the law of concentration and centralization of capital inevitably led to the victory of large and large enterprises, in comparison with which small and medium-sized enterprises play an increasingly subordinate role. In turn, the concentration of production prepared the transition from the rule of free competition to the rule of monopolies.

In Germany, in enterprises with more than 50 employees, in 1882, 22% of all workers and employees were concentrated, in 1895 - 30, in 1907 - 37, in 1925 - 47.2, in 1939 - 49.9%. The share of the largest enterprises (with more than a thousand employees) in the entire industry grew from 1907 to 1925: in terms of the number of employees - from 9.6 to 13.3%, in terms of engine power - from 32 to 41.1%.

In the United States of America in 1904, the largest enterprises with a production worth a million dollars or more accounted for 0.9% of the total number of enterprises; 25.6% of the total number of workers were employed at these enterprises, and they provided 38% of the total gross industrial output. In 1909, the largest enterprises, accounting for 1.1% of the total number of enterprises, had 30.5% of all employed workers and provided 43.8% of the total gross industrial output. In 1939, the largest enterprises, accounting for 5.2% of the total number of enterprises, concentrated 55% of all employed workers and 67.5% of the total industrial output.

Russian industry was distinguished by a high degree of concentration . In Russia in 1879, large enterprises (with more than 100 workers) accounted for 4.4% of all enterprises and concentrated 54.8% of the total production. In 1903, 76.6% of all industrial workers were concentrated in large enterprises, and they provided the overwhelming majority of industrial output. The concentration of production proceeds most rapidly in heavy industry and in the new branches of industry (chemical, electrical engineering, automotive, etc.), lagging behind in light industry, in which there are many small and medium-sized enterprises in all capitalist countries.

One of the forms of concentration of production is a combination, that is, the combination in one enterprise of different types of production, which are either successive stages of processing raw materials (for example, metallurgical plants that combine ore mining, iron and steel smelting, production of rolled products), or playing an auxiliary role alone. in relation to another (for example, the use of production waste). The combination gives large enterprises an even greater advantage in the competition.

At a certain stage of its development, the concentration of production leads close to monopoly. Large enterprises require huge masses of profit in order to withstand the fierce competition with the same giants and be able to further expand production, and high profits are ensured only by monopoly dominance in the market. On the other hand, it is easier for a few dozen giant enterprises to come to an agreement among themselves than for hundreds and thousands of small enterprises. Thus, free competition is replaced by monopoly. This is the economic essence of imperialism.

A monopoly is an agreement, alliance or association of capitalists who have concentrated in their hands the production and marketing of a significant part of the output of one or several industries in order to establish high prices for goods and obtain monopoly high profits.

The simplest forms of monopoly are short-term sales price agreements. They have various names: conventions, corners, rings, etc. More developed forms of monopoly are cartels, syndicates, trusts, and concerns.

A cartel is a monopolistic union whose members agree on the terms of sale, terms of payment, divide sales markets among themselves, determine the quantity of goods produced, and set prices. The quantity of goods that each of the cartel members is entitled to produce and sell is called a quota; for violation of the quota, a fine is paid to the cashier of the cartel.

A syndicate is a monopoly organization in which the sale of goods and sometimes the purchase of raw materials are carried out by a common office. Trust is a monopoly in which the ownership of all enterprises is combined, and their owners have become shareholders who receive a profit according to the number of shares or shares they own. At the head of the trust is the board, which manages all production, marketing of products and finances of formerly independent enterprises. Trusts are often included in larger unions - concerns. A concern is an association of a number of enterprises in various branches of industry, trading firms, banks, transport, and insurance companies on the basis of a common financial dependence on a certain group of the largest capitalists.

The monopolies occupy commanding heights in the economies of the capitalist countries. They embraced heavy industry, as well as many branches of light industry, railway and water transport, banks, domestic and foreign trade, and established their oppression over agriculture.

The ferrous metallurgy of the United States of America is dominated by eight monopolies, which in 1952 controlled 84% of the country's total steel production capacity; of these, the two largest - the American Steel Trust and the Bethlehem Steel Corporation - had 51% of the total production capacity. The oldest monopoly in the United States is the Standard Oil Trust. In the automotive industry, three firms are of decisive importance: General Motors, Ford, and Chrysler. The electrical industry is dominated by two firms: General Electric and Westinghouse. The chemical industry is controlled by the Dupont de Nemours concern, and the aluminum industry by the Mellon concern.

In England, the role of monopoly associations increased especially after the First World War, when cartels arose in the textile and coal industries, in ferrous metallurgy, and in a number of new branches of industry. The English Chemical Trust controls about nine-tenths of all basic chemicals, about two-fifths of all dyes, and nearly all of the country's nitrogen production. He is closely connected with the most important branches of British industry, and especially with military concerns.

In Germany, cartels have become widespread since the end of the last century. Between the two world wars, the country's economy was dominated by the Steel Trust ("Vereinigte

Stalwerke"), which had about 200 thousand workers and employees, the Chemical Trust ("Interessen Gemeinschaft Farbenindustry") with 100 thousand workers and employees, the monopoly of the coal industry, the cannon concern Krupp, electrical concerns "General Electricity Company" and "Siemens".

In France, Japan , and even in such small countries as Belgium, Sweden, Switzerland, monopoly organizations occupy commanding positions in industry.

In Russia, the big monopolies primarily embraced the main branches of heavy industry. The syndicate "Prodamet" (an association for the sale of products of metallurgical enterprises), which arose in 1902, controlled the sale of more than four-fifths of ferrous metal. In 1904, the Prodvagon syndicate was organized, which almost completely monopolized the production and sale of wagons. The same syndicate united locomotive factories. The syndicate "Produgol" was created in 1904 by the largest coal enterprises of the Donbass, owned by Franco-Belgian capital; it covered three-quarters of all coal production in the Donbass.

Bourgeois economists, trying to embellish modern capitalism, assert that the spread of monopolies leads to a cure in the bourgeois system of such evils as competition, anarchy of production, and crises. In fact, not only is imperialism unable to eliminate competition, anarchy in production, and crises, but it sharpens all the contradictions of capitalism even more.

Lenin pointed out that imperialism cannot rebuild capitalism from top to bottom. With the dominant role of monopolies in all capitalist countries, numerous medium and small enterprises, and masses of small producers—peasants and artisans—are preserved.

The monopoly that is being created in some branches of industry increases the chaotic nature of capitalist production as a whole. Not only is competition not eliminated, but it is taking even more acute forms.

First, competition does not stop within monopolies. Members of syndicates and cartels fight among themselves for the most profitable markets, for a large share (quota) of production and sales. In trusts and concerns there is a struggle for leading positions, for controlling blocks of shares, for the distribution of profits.

Secondly, competition is conducted between monopolies: both between monopolies of the same industry, and between monopolies of different industries that supply goods to each other (for example, steel and automobile trusts) or produce goods that can replace each other (coal, oil , electricity). Given the limited capacity of the domestic market, the monopolies producing consumer goods are waging a fierce struggle for the sale of their goods.

Thirdly, competition occurs between monopolies and non-monopolized enterprises. Monopolized industries are in a privileged position in relation to other industries. The monopolies take every measure to stifle "foreign", "wild" enterprises that do not belong to monopoly associations.

"Monopolies, growing out of free competition, do not eliminate it, but exist above it and next to it, thereby giving rise to a number of especially sharp and sharp contradictions, frictions, conflicts" [2] . The dominance of monopolies gives the competitive struggle a particularly destructive and predatory character. Monopolies use all possible methods of direct violence, bribery and blackmail, resort to complex financial fraud.

The dominance of monopolies means a further deepening of the basic contradiction of capitalism - the contradiction between the social character of production and the private capitalist form of appropriation, as a result of which crises become even more devastating.

Concentration and monopolies in banking. The new role of banks.

The idea of the real strength and significance of modern monopolies cannot be sufficiently complete without taking into account the role of banks. In banking, as in industry, there is a concentration of capital and a transition from free competition to monopoly. Initially, banks served mainly as intermediaries in payments. With the development of capitalism, the activities of banks as merchants of capital expanded. The accumulation of capital and the concentration of production in industry have led to the concentration of huge free funds in banks, looking for a profitable application. The share of large banks in the total mass of banking turnover has been steadily growing.

During the 33 years before the First World War (1880-1913), the growth in deposits in the banking systems of the four largest capitalist states - the United States of America, Germany, England, and France - alone amounted to 127 billion marks. Since then, the growth of deposits has been even faster; in a period twice as short, from 1913 to 1928, deposits in these countries increased by 183 billion marks.

In the United States of America , the 20 largest banks accounted for 15% in 1900, 19% in 1929, 27% in 1939, and 29% in 1952 of the total amount of deposits in all US banks. In England, the sum of the balance sheets of the five largest banks in 1900 was 28%; in 1916, 37; in 1929, 73; and in 1952, 79% of the total balances of all English depository banks. In France , the six deposit banks in 1952 accounted for 66% of the total deposits in all French banks. In Germany on the eve of the First World War, about half of the deposits available in all German banks were concentrated in large Berlin banks, and in 1929-1932. - two-thirds.

Concentration in banking, as in industry, leads to monopoly. The largest banks, through the purchase of shares, the provision of credit, etc., subjugate the small ones. Having seized a monopoly position, large banks enter into agreements among themselves on the division of spheres of influence. Monopoly unions of banks are formed. Each such union commands dozens and sometimes hundreds of smaller banks, which actually become branches of large ones. Through a developed network of branches, large banks collect funds from many enterprises in their cash desks. Almost the entire money capital of the capitalist class and the savings of other sections of the population fall into the hands of small groups of bank tycoons.

The concentration of industry and the formation of banking monopolies lead to a significant change in the relationship between banks and industry. With the increase in the size of enterprises, large, long-term loans extended by banks to industrial capitalists become increasingly important. The growth in the mass of deposits at the disposal of banks opens up wide possibilities for such a long-term investment of bank funds in industry. The most common form of investing bank money in industry is the purchase of shares in various enterprises. Banks contribute to the formation of joint-stock enterprises by taking over the reorganization of the enterprises of individual capitalists into joint-stock companies and the creation of new joint-stock companies (foundation).

From modest intermediaries, banks are turning into all-powerful money market monopolists. The interests of banks and industrial enterprises are intertwined ever more closely. When a bank finances several large enterprises in a certain industry, it is interested in a monopoly agreement between them and promotes such an agreement. In this way, banks greatly intensify and accelerate the process of concentration of capital and the formation of monopolies.

Financial capital and financial oligarchy.

As a result of the fact that banks become co-owners of industrial, commercial, transport enterprises, acquiring their shares and bonds, and industrial monopolies, in turn, own shares of banks associated with them, there is an interweaving of monopoly banking and industrial capital, a new type of capital arises - financial capital. Finance capital is the fused capital of banking and industrial monopolies. The era of imperialism is the era of finance capital.

Defining financial capital, Lenin emphasized three most important points: "Concentration of production; the monopolies that grow out of it; the merging or merging of banks with industry - this is the history of the emergence of finance capital and the content of this concept" [3] .

The merging of banking capital with industrial capital is clearly manifested in the personal union of the leaders of banking and industrial monopolies. The same persons head the largest monopoly associations in banking, industry, trade, and other branches of the capitalist economy.

In Germany, before the First World War, the six largest Berlin banks had their proteges as directors in 344 industrial enterprises and as board members in another 407, for a total of 751 companies. On the other hand, the governing bodies of these six banks included 51 major industrialists. In the future, this personal union was further developed. In 1932, the governing bodies of the three main Berlin banks included 70 of the largest representatives of industry. In the United States of America in 1950, a narrow group of 400 industrialists and bankers occupied one-third of the 3,705 directorial positions in the 250 largest corporations (joint-stock companies) that owned 42% of the country's capital.

In every capitalist country, small handfuls of the biggest bankers and monopoly industrialists hold in their hands all the vital branches of the economy, disposing of the overwhelming mass of social wealth. The management of capitalist monopolies inevitably becomes the rule of a financial oligarchy (the Greek word "oligarchy" literally means "the rule of a few"). Imperialism is characterized by the omnipotence of monopoly trusts and syndicates, banks, and financial oligarchy in the industrial countries.

The domination of the financial oligarchy in the economic field is carried out primarily through the so-called "participation system". It consists in the fact that a large financial businessman or a group of businessmen holds in his hands the main joint-stock company ("mother company") that heads the concern; this company, in turn, owning controlling stakes, dominates the "subsidiaries" dependent on it; they manage in a similar way in "grandchildren societies", etc. Through this system, financial tycoons get the opportunity to dispose of huge amounts of foreign capital.

With the help of a widely ramified system of participation, the eight largest US financial groups - Morgan, Rockefeller, Kuhn-Loeb, Mellon, DuPont, Chicago, Cleveland, and Boston - dominate the entire economy of the country. Morgan's sphere of influence by 1948 covered banks and corporations with a total capital of 55 billion dollars, Rockefeller - 26.7 billion, Du Pont - 6.5 billion, Mellon - 6 billion dollars.

The financial oligarchy, which enjoys a virtual monopoly, receives huge and ever-growing masses of profits from the foundation (that is, the creation of joint-stock companies), from the issuance of shares and bonds, from the placement of state loans, from profitable state orders. Financial capital, concentrated in a few hands, collects ever-increasing tribute from society.

The export of capital.

For pre-monopoly capitalism, with the dominance of free competition, the export of goods was typical. For imperialist capitalism, with the dominance of monopolies, the export of capital has become typical.

On the threshold of the 20th century, in the richest countries, where the accumulation of capital reached enormous proportions, there was a huge "surplus of capital".

Capital is "surplus" mainly for two reasons. First, the miserable standard of living of the masses puts up obstacles to the further growth of production. Secondly, the lag of agriculture behind industry and, in general, the uneven development of various sectors of the economy is becoming more and more intensified. If capitalism could raise agriculture, raise the standard of living of the working masses, then there could be no question of any "surplus of capital".

But then capitalism would not be capitalism, for both the uneven development and the semi-starvation standard of living of the masses of the population are the fundamental conditions and prerequisites for this mode of production. The surplus of capital in the capitalist developed countries is thus of a relative nature. The need for the export of capital is created by the fact that in a few countries capitalism is "overripe", and capital lacks (given the underdevelopment of agriculture and the poverty of the masses) the field of "profitable" premises"[4].

In pursuit of maximum profit, "surplus" capital rushes abroad. Capital is mainly exported to backward countries, where capital is scarce, wages are low, raw materials are cheap, and the price of land is comparatively low. In these countries, monopoly capital has the opportunity to receive, and indeed receives, huge profits.

Along with the backward countries, capital is also exported to the industrialized countries. This takes place during a period of particularly rapid development of such countries, which calls for an influx of capital from outside (for example, the United States before the First World War), or in an environment of their weakening caused by the war (Germany after the First World War, the Western European capitalist countries after the Second World War).

The export of capital takes place in two main forms: in the form of loan capital and in the form of productive capital. The export of loan capital takes place when loans are granted to governments, cities, banks of other countries. The export of productive capital is carried out through the creation of industrial enterprises abroad, concessions, the construction of railways, and also by buying up for a pittance already existing enterprises in countries that have weakened (for example, as a result of the war).

Bourgeois economists and politicians portray the export of capital as "aid" and "benefits" allegedly rendered by developed capitalist countries to backward peoples. In fact, the export of capital, while accelerating the development of capitalist relations in backward countries, at the same time leads to the all-round enslavement and plunder of these countries by foreign monopolies.

The export of capital is closely connected with the growth of the export of goods. Foreign monopolies seize markets and sources of raw materials in debtor countries. Thus, the export of capital is one of the foundations of a system of imperialist oppression in which a few rich usurer countries exploit most of the world. The world has been divided into a handful of usurer states and a vast majority of debtor states.

The export of capital has serious consequences for the countries exporting capital. These countries, on the one hand, increase their wealth and strengthen their positions in the world market. They receive from outside a constant influx of surplus value in the form of interest on loans or profits from foreign enterprises. On the other hand, often there is a stagnation in the own industrial development of the country exporting capital. One of the important results of the export of capital is the growth of rivalry between the powers, the struggle for the most profitable areas for the investment of capital.

Before the First World War, the main exporting countries were England, France, and Germany. Their investments abroad amounted to 175 - 200 billion francs: England - 75 - 100 billion, France - 60 billion, Germany - 44 billion francs. The export of capital from the United States has not yet played a major role, amounting to less than 10 billion francs.

After the war of 1914-1918 there have been major changes in world capital exports. Germany lost its capital abroad. The foreign investments of England and France were significantly reduced, and the export of capital from the United States increased greatly. In 1929, the USA almost equaled Britain in terms of the size of its foreign investments. After the Second World War, the export of capital from the United States increased even more.

The economic division of the world between the unions of capitalists. international monopolies.

As the export of capital grows, as foreign ties expand and the "spheres of influence" of the largest monopolies expand, conditions are created for dividing the world market between them. International monopolies are formed.

International monopolies are agreements between the largest monopolies of various countries on the division of markets, price policy, and the size of production. The formation of international monopolies signifies a new stage in the concentration of production and capital, incomparably higher than the previous ones.

Defenders of international monopolies try to present them as an instrument of peace, asserting that international agreements between monopolists can peacefully settle the contradictions that arise between imperialist groups and countries. Such statements have nothing to do with reality. In fact, the economic division of the world by international monopolies takes place depending on the strength of the parties, while the strength of individual monopoly groups varies. Each of them is incessantly fighting to increase its share, to expand the sphere of monopoly exploitation. Changes in the balance of power inevitably entail an intensification of the struggle for the redistribution of markets, an aggravation of contradictions between various groups and the states that support them. The international agreements of the monopolists are notable for their fragility and contain the source of inevitable conflicts.

International monopolies began to emerge in the 1860s and 1880s. By the end of the last century, their total number did not exceed 40. On the eve of the First World War, there were about 100 international cartels throughout the world, and before the Second World War, their number exceeded 300.

Even before the First World War, the oil market was actually divided between the American trust Standard Oil, which was in the hands of Rockefeller, and the Royal-Dutch-Shell concern, with the predominant influence of British capital.

The market for electrical products was divided between two monopoly firms: the German General Electric Company and the American General Electric Corporation, controlled by the Morgan group.

International monopolistic agreements even covered such areas as the production of weapons. The largest arms manufacturers - Armstrong-Vickers in England, Schneider-Creusot in France, Krupp in Germany, Bofors in Sweden - have been linked together by many threads for a long time.
The international monopolies played a big role in the preparations for the Second World War. The largest monopolies of the United States, Britain, and France, bound by cartel agreements with German trusts, inspired and directed the policy of the ruling circles of these countries, the policy of

encouraging and inciting Hitlerite aggression, which led to war.

Completion of the territorial division of the world between the great powers and the struggle for its redistribution.

Along with and in connection with the economic division of the world between capitalist alliances, there is a territorial division of the world between bourgeois states, a struggle for colonies, a struggle to seize foreign lands.

Colonies are called countries deprived of state independence and constituting the possessions of imperialist metropolitan states. In the epoch of imperialism, there are also various types of dependent countries - semi-colonies. Semi-colonies are called countries that are formally independent, but in reality are politically and economically dependent on the imperialist states.

The defenders of the bourgeoisie portray imperialist rule over the colonies as a "civilizing mission" supposedly aimed at leading the backward peoples onto the path of progress and independent development. In fact, imperialism dooms colonial and dependent countries to economic backwardness, and hundreds of millions of the population of these countries to unprecedented oppression and bondage, lack of rights and poverty, hunger, and ignorance. The seizure of the colonies by the imperialist powers leads to an unprecedented intensification of national oppression and racial discrimination. According to Lenin, capitalism, from being a liberator of nations, as it was during the period of struggle against feudalism, at the stage of imperialism has turned into a monstrous oppressor of nations.

Back in the middle of the 18th century, England enslaved India - a country with the richest natural resources and a population that is many times larger than the population of the metropolis. In the middle of the 19th century, the United States of America seized vast territories from neighboring Mexico, and in the following decades established its dominance over a number of countries in Latin America.

In the 60s and 70s of the last century, the colonial possessions of European countries still occupied a relatively small part of overseas lands. In 1876, only one tenth of the territory of Africa was occupied by the colonies of European countries. About half of the Asian continent and the islands of the Pacific Ocean (Polynesia) have not yet been captured by the capitalist states.

In the last quarter of the 19th century, the map of the world underwent fundamental changes. Following the oldest colonial power, England, all the developed capitalist countries embarked on the path of territorial conquest. France by the end of the 19th century had become a major colonial power with possessions of 3.7 million square miles. Germany captured a million square miles of territory with 14.7 million people, Belgium - 900 thousand square miles with 30 million people, the United States captured the most important stronghold in the Pacific Ocean - the Philippine Islands, as well as Cuba, Puerto Rico, Guam, the Hawaiian Islands, the island Samoa, established their actual dominance over a number of countries in Central and South America.

From 1876 to 1914, the so-called "great powers" captured about 25 million square kilometers of territory, which is one and a half times the area of the metropolitan countries. A number of countries were placed in conditions of semi-colonial dependence on imperialist states: China, with a population of almost one-fourth of all mankind, as well as Turkey and Persia (Iran). By the beginning of the First World War, more than half of humanity was under the rule of the colonial powers.

The imperialists establish and maintain their power over the colonies through methods of deceit and violence, using the superiority of their military technology. The history of colonial policy is a continuous chain of wars of conquest and punitive expeditions against enslaved peoples, as well as bloody conflicts between countries that own colonies. Lenin called the war of the United States against Spain in 1898 the first war of the imperialist type, which marked the beginning of the era of imperialist wars. The uprising of the Filipino people against the invaders was brutally suppressed by American troops.

England, which created the largest colonial empire, for more than two centuries waged uninterrupted wars of extermination against the population of the occupied countries of Asia and Africa. The history of colonial seizures by Germany, France, Japan, Italy, and other countries is full of cruelties.

By the beginning of the 20th century, the division of the world was completed. The colonial policy of the capitalist countries led to the seizure of all lands not occupied by the imperialists. There are no more "free" lands left, a situation has arisen in which each new seizure involves taking the territory from its owner. The completion of the division of the world put the struggle for its redivision on the queue. The struggle for the redistribution of the already divided world is one of the main distinguishing features of monopoly capitalism. This struggle eventually turns into a struggle for world domination and inevitably leads to imperialist wars on a world scale.

Imperialist wars and the arms race bring enormous hardships to the peoples of all capitalist countries and cost millions of human lives. At the same time, wars and the militarization of the economy are a source of income for the monopolies, giving them particularly high profits.

Basic economic law of monopoly capitalism.

As already mentioned, the economic essence of imperialism lies in the replacement of free competition by the domination of monopolies. Monopolies, setting monopoly prices, set as their goal, according to Lenin's definition, obtaining monopoly high profits, which significantly exceed the average profit. The receipt of high monopoly profits by the monopolies follows from the very essence of imperialism and is ensured by the unprecedented intensification of the exploitation by the monopolies of the working class, the robbery of the peasantry and other small commodity producers, the export of capital to backward countries and the draining of all the vital juices from these countries, colonial conquests, imperialist wars, which are a golden mine for monopolies. In the works of Lenin, devoted to the disclosure of the economic and political essence of imperialism, given the initial provisions of the basic economic law of modern capitalism. Based on these initial propositions of Lenin, Stalin formulated the basic economic law of modern capitalism.

The main features and requirements of the basic economic law of monopoly capitalism are as follows:

> "ensuring the maximum capitalist profit through the exploitation, ruin and impoverishment of the majority of the population of a given country, through the enslavement and systematic robbery of the peoples of other countries, especially backward countries, and finally, through wars and the militarization of the national economy used to ensure the highest profits." [5]

Thus, the basic economic law of capitalism - the law of surplus value - in the period of imperialism receives its further development and concretization. Whereas under pre-monopoly capitalism the dominance of free competition led to an equalization of the rate of profit of individual capitalists, under imperialism the monopolies ensure for themselves a monopolistically high, maximum profit. It is the maximum profit that is the engine of monopoly capitalism.

The objective conditions for obtaining maximum profits are created by the establishment of the dominance of monopolies in certain branches of production. At the stage of imperialism, the concentration and centralization of capital reach its highest degree. Because of this, the expansion of production requires huge capital investments. On the other hand, during the period of monopoly capitalism, a fierce competitive struggle unfolds between gigantic enterprises. In this struggle, the strongest monopolies win, having the largest capitals and receiving the maximum profits.

Due to the maximum profits, the monopolies are able to carry out expanded reproduction and ensure their dominance in the capitalist world. The pursuit of maximum profit by the monopolies leads to an extreme aggravation of all the contradictions of capitalism.

The general basis of the maximum profit of the capitalist monopolies, as of all capitalist profit, is the surplus value squeezed out of the workers by exploiting them in the process of production. The exploitation of the working class is increased by the monopolies to an extreme degree. Through the use of all kinds of sweatshop systems of organizing and remunerating labor, an uninterrupted, debilitating intensification of labor is achieved, which means, first of all, a huge increase in the rate and mass of surplus value squeezed out of the workers. Further, the intensification of labor leads to the fact that many workers are redundant and fall into the ranks of the army of unemployed, deprived of any hope of returning to the production process. All workers are also thrown out of enterprises, for whom excessive acceleration of production processes is unbearable.

In the USA, the rate of surplus value in the mining and manufacturing industries, calculated on the basis of official data, was 145% in 1889, 165% in 1919, 210% in 1929, and 220% in 1939. Thus, in 40 years the rate of surplus-value has increased $1 > 1/2$ times .

At the same time, real wages are steadily declining as a result of the rising cost of living. Rising prices for livelihoods, the increasing burden of the tax burden and inflation further reduce the real earnings of the worker. In the era of imperialism, the gap between the wages of the worker and the value of his labor power increases enormously. This signifies an even more drastic effect of the general law of capitalist accumulation, which causes the relative and absolute impoverishment of the proletariat. The growth of the exploitation of the working class in the process of production is complemented by the plundering of the working people as consumers; the workers have to overpay large sums to the monopolies, which charge high monopoly prices for the goods they produce and sell.

Under conditions of monopoly capitalism, goods produced by the monopolies are no longer sold at production prices, but at much higher—monopoly—prices.

Monopoly price equals production costs plus maximum profit, which is much higher than the average rate of profit; the monopoly price is higher than the price of production and, as a rule, exceeds the cost of goods. At the same time, the monopoly price, as Marx pointed out, cannot destroy the boundaries determined by the cost of goods. The high level of monopoly prices does not change the total amount of value produced in the world capitalist economy and surplus value: what the monopolies gain, the workers, small producers, and the population of dependent countries lose. One of the sources of maximum profit that monopolies receive is the redistribution of surplus value, as a result of which non-monopolized enterprises often do not even gain an average profit. By maintaining prices at a high level that exceeds the cost of goods, monopolies appropriate the results of the growth of labor productivity and the reduction of production costs. Thus they levy ever-increasing tribute on the population.

The customs policy of the bourgeois states is an important instrument of monopolistic inflation of prices. In the era of free competition, high customs duties were resorted to mainly by weaker countries. whose industries needed protection from foreign competition. In the epoch of imperialism, on the contrary, high duties serve as a means for the monopolies to attack, to fight for the capture of new markets. High duties help maintain monopoly prices within the country.

In order to conquer new foreign markets, monopolies widely use dumping - sale. goods abroad at bargain prices, well below domestic market prices, and often even below production costs. Expansion of sales abroad in the form of dumping makes it possible to maintain high prices within the country without reducing production, and the losses caused by junk exports are covered by rising prices in the domestic market. After this external market has been conquered and assigned to the monopolies, they go over to selling goods at high monopoly prices.

The exploitation of the bulk of the peasantry by the monopolies is expressed primarily in the fact that the domination of the monopolies gives rise to a growing discrepancy between the level of prices for agricultural products and industrial goods (the so-called "scissors" of prices): while selling goods at artificially inflated prices, the monopolies at the same time buy the peasants have the products of their farms at extremely low prices. Being a tool for draining funds from agriculture, monopoly prices retard its development. One of the strongest levers for the ruin of peasant farms is the development of mortgage credit. The monopolies entangle the peasants in debts and then appropriate their land and property for next to nothing.

The purchase by the monopolies of the products of the peasant economy at extremely low prices does not at all mean that the urban consumer enjoys cheap foodstuffs. Between the peasant and the urban consumer are intermediaries - merchants united in monopoly organizations that ruin the peasants and rob the urban consumers.

"Capitalism," wrote M. Thorez in his work "The Policy of the Communist Party in the Countryside," managed to turn small peasant property - parcels, on which peasants sometimes work 14-16 hours a day - not into a means of subsistence and prosperity for working peasants, but as a tool for their exploitation and enslavement. Through mortgages, through the machinations of financial pirates, through high taxes and extortions, high rents, and especially through competition from large landowners - capitalists, the bourgeoisie ruins the middle and small peasants.

Further, the source of the maximum profits of the monopolies is the enslavement and plunder of the economically backward and dependent countries by the bourgeoisie of the imperialist states. The systematic plunder of the colonies and other backward countries, the transformation of a number of independent countries into dependent countries, are an inalienable feature of monopoly capitalism. Imperialism cannot live and develop without a continuous influx of tribute from the foreign countries it plunders.

The monopolies receive huge profits primarily from their investments in colonial and dependent countries. These revenues are the result of the most cruel and inhuman exploitation of the working masses of the colonial world. The monopolies profit by unequal exchange, that is, by selling their commodities in colonial and dependent countries at prices far exceeding their value, and by buying up commodities produced in these countries at exorbitantly low prices that do not cover their value. Along with this, the monopolies receive high profits from the colonies in transport, insurance, and banking operations.

Finally, wars and the militarization of the economy are a source of profit for the monopolies. Wars enrich the magnates of finance capital enormously, and in the intervals between wars the monopolies strive to maintain a high level of their profits by means of an unrestrained arms race. Wars and the militarization of the economy bring rich military orders to the monopolists, paid for by the treasury at inflated prices, and an abundant stream of loans and subsidies from the state budget. Enterprises working for the war are placed in exceptionally advantageous conditions with respect to the supply of raw materials, production materials and labor force. All labor laws are abolished, workers are declared mobilized, strikes are prohibited. All this makes it possible for the capitalists to raise the degree of exploitation to the extreme by bringing the intensity of labor to the highest limits.

Thus, the militarization of the capitalist economy, both in war and in peacetime, means a sharp increase in the exploitation of the working masses in the interests of increasing the maximum profits of the monopolies.

The basic economic law of modern capitalism, determining the entire course of development of capitalism at its imperialist stage, makes it possible to understand and explain the inevitability of growth and the aggravation of the insoluble contradictions inherent in it.

SUMMARY

1. Imperialism, or monopoly capitalism, is the highest and last stage in the development of the capitalist mode of production. The transition from pre-monopoly capitalism to monopoly capitalism took place during the last third of the 19th century. Imperialism finally took shape by the beginning of the 20th century.

2. The main economic features of imperialism are: 1) the concentration of production and capital, which has reached such a high stage of development that it has created monopolies that play a decisive role in economic life; 2) the merging of banking capital with industrial capital and the formation on this basis of finance capital, of a financial oligarchy; 3) the export of capital, in contrast to the export of goods, is of particular importance; 4) international monopoly unions of capitalists are formed, dividing the world among themselves; 5) the territorial division of the land by the major imperialist powers has been completed. The completion of the economic division of the world leads to a struggle for its redistribution, which inevitably gives rise to imperialist wars on a world scale.

3. The basic economic law of monopoly capitalism consists in securing maximum capitalist profits by exploiting, ruining, and

impoverishing the majority of the population of a given country, by enslaving and systematically plundering the peoples of other countries, especially backward countries, and finally, by wars and the militarization of the national economy.

[1] V. I. Lenin, Imperialism, as the highest stage of capitalism, Works, vol. 22, p. 253.

[2] V. I. Lenin, Imperialism as the highest stage of capitalism, Works, vol. 22, p. 253.

[3] V. I. Lenin, Imperialism, as the highest stage of capitalism, Works, vol. 22, p. 214.

[4] V. I. Lenin, Imperialism, as the highest stage of capitalism, Works, vol. 22, p. 229.

[5] I. V. Stalin, Economic problems of socialism in the USSR, p. 38.

The historical place of imperialism

Imperialism is the last stage of capitalism.

Determining the historical place of imperialism in relation to capitalism in general, Lenin wrote: "Imperialism is a special historical stage of capitalism. This feature is threefold: imperialism is (1) monopoly capitalism; (2) parasitic or decaying capitalism; (3) – dying capitalism" [1] .

Monopoly capitalism does not and cannot eliminate the foundations of the old capitalism. It is in a sense a superstructure over the old, pre-monopoly capitalism, which is everywhere combined with pre-capitalist forms of economy. Just as there is not and cannot be "pure capitalism", the existence of "pure imperialism" is inconceivable. Even in the most developed countries, along with monopolies, there are many small and medium-sized enterprises, especially in light industry, agriculture, trade, and other branches of the economy. In almost all capitalist countries, a significant part of the population is made up of the peasantry, which for the most part leads a simple commodity economy. The vast majority of mankind lives in colonial and semi-colonial countries, where imperialist oppression is intertwined with pre-capitalist, especially feudal, forms of exploitation.

An essential feature of imperialism is that monopolies exist side by side with exchange, the market, competition, and crises. It follows from this that at the monopoly stage of capitalism, the economic laws of capitalism in general remain in full force, but their actions are determined by the basic economic law of modern capitalism - the law of ensuring the maximum capitalist profit. Therefore, they act with increased destructive power. This is how matters stand with the laws of value and surplus value, with the law of competition and anarchy of production, with the general law of capitalist accumulation, which causes the relative and absolute impoverishment of the working class and dooms the bulk of the working peasantry to impoverishment and ruin, with the contradictions of capitalist reproduction, economic crises.

The monopolies bring the socialization of production to the limit possible under capitalism. Large and largest enterprises, each employing thousands of people, produce a significant proportion of all products in the most important industries. The monopolies tie gigantic enterprises together, take into account markets, sources of raw materials, seize scientific personnel, inventions, and improvements. The big banks control almost all of the country's money. The ties between the various sectors of the economy and their interdependence are growing enormously. Industry, possessing gigantic production capacities, is capable of rapidly increasing the mass of goods produced.

At the same time, the means of production remain the private property of the capitalists. The decisive part of the means of production is at the disposal of the monopolies. In the pursuit of maximum profit, the monopolies in every way increase the degree of exploitation of the working class, which leads to a sharp increase in the impoverishment of the working masses and a decrease in their purchasing power.

Thus, the domination of monopolies to the greatest extent exacerbates the basic contradiction of capitalism—the contradiction between the social character of production and the private capitalist form of appropriation of the results of production. It is becoming more and more apparent that the social character of the production process requires social ownership of the means of production.

In the era of imperialism, the productive forces of society have reached such a level of development that they do not fit within the narrow framework of capitalist production relations. Capitalism, which replaced feudalism as a more progressive mode of production, turned into a reactionary force at the imperialist stage, hindering the development of human society. The economic law of the obligatory correspondence of production relations to the nature of the productive forces requires the replacement of capitalist production relations by new, socialist ones. This law meets with the strongest opposition from the ruling classes, and above all from the monopoly bourgeoisie and big landowners, who seek to prevent the working class from forming an alliance with the peasantry and overthrowing the bourgeois system.

The high level of development of the productive forces and the socialization of production, the extreme aggravation of all the contradictions of bourgeois society testify to the fact that capitalism, having entered the last stage of its development, is fully ripe for its replacement by the highest social system - socialism.

Imperialism is parasitic or decaying capitalism.

Imperialism is parasitic or decaying capitalism. The tendency to stagnation and decay is inevitably generated by the dominance of monopolies, striving to obtain maximum profits. Monopolies, insofar as they are able to dictate prices in the market and artificially maintain them at a high level, are by no means always interested in applying technical innovations. Monopolies often hinder technical progress; they keep under wraps the largest scientific discoveries and technical inventions for years.

Thus, monopolies tend to stagnate and decay, and under certain conditions this tendency prevails. This circumstance, however, by no means ruled out the relatively rapid growth of capitalism before the Second World War. But this growth was extremely uneven, falling further and further behind the enormous possibilities opened up by modern science and technology.

Modern highly developed technology puts forward grandiose tasks, the fulfillment of which is beyond the capacity of decaying capitalism. Not a single capitalist country, for example, can make extensive use of its hydropower resources because of the obstacles posed by private ownership of land and the dominance of monopolies. The capitalist countries are not in a position to use the possibilities of modern science and technology to carry out extensive work to improve soil fertility. The interests of the capitalist monopolies hinder the use of atomic energy for peaceful purposes.

"Wherever you turn," V. I. Lenin wrote back in 1913, "at every step you meet tasks that humanity is quite capable of solving immediately, capitalism prevents. He accumulated heaps of wealth - and made people slaves of this wealth. He solved the most difficult problems of technology - and stalled the implementation of technical improvements because of the poverty and ignorance of millions of the population, because of the stupid stinginess of a handful of millionaires " [2] .

The decay of capitalism is expressed in the growth of parasitism. The capitalist class loses all connection with the production process. The management of enterprises is concentrated in the hands of hired technical personnel. The overwhelming majority of the bourgeoisie and landlords are turning into rentiers - people who own securities and live on the income from these securities (coupon clipping). The parasitic consumption of the exploiting classes is growing.

The complete isolation of the rentier stratum from production is further intensified by the export of capital and income from foreign investment. The export of capital leaves the mark of parasitism on the whole country, which lives by the exploitation of the peoples of other countries and colonies. The capital exported abroad constitutes an ever-increasing share of the national wealth of the imperialist countries, and the income from these capitals constitutes an ever-increasing part of the income of the capitalist class. Lenin called the export of capital parasitism squared.

The capital placed abroad in 1929 was in relation to the national wealth: in England - 18%, in France - 15%, in Holland - about 20%, in Belgium and Switzerland - 12% each. In 1929, the income from capital invested abroad exceeded the income from foreign trade: in England - more than 7 times, in the United States - 5 times.

In the United States of America, the income of rentiers from securities in 1913 amounted to 1.8 billion dollars, and in 1931 - 8.1 billion dollars, which is 1.4 times the entire gross cash income of 30 million farming population in the same year. The USA is a country where the parasitic features of modern capitalism, as well as the predatory nature of imperialism, are most pronounced.

The parasitic character of capitalism is clearly manifested in the fact that a number of bourgeois countries are turning into rentier states. By means of enslaving loans, the largest imperialist countries extract huge profits from the debtor countries and subjugate them economically and politically. The rentier state is the state of parasitic, decaying capitalism. The exploitation of the colonies and dependent countries, which is one of the main sources of the maximum profits of the monopolies, turns a handful of the richest capitalist countries into parasites on the body of the rest of mankind.

The parasitic character of capitalism finds its expression in the growth of militarism. An ever-increasing share of the national income, and chiefly the income of the working people, is taken into the state budget and spent on the upkeep of huge armies, on the preparation and conduct of imperialist wars. Being one of the most important methods of ensuring maximum profits for the monopolies, the militarization of the economy and imperialist wars mean at the same time the rapacious destruction of many human lives and enormous material values.

The intensification of parasitism is inextricably linked with the fact that gigantic masses of people are torn away from socially useful labor. The army of the unemployed is growing, the number of people employed in the service of the exploiting classes in the state apparatus, as well as in the incredibly swollen sphere of circulation, is increasing.

The decay of capitalism is further manifested in the fact that the imperialist bourgeoisie, using its profits from the exploitation of the colonies and dependent countries, systematically bribes, through higher wages and other handouts, a small elite of skilled workers - the so-called labor aristocracy. With the support of the bourgeoisie, the labor aristocracy seizes command posts in the trade unions; along with the petty-bourgeois elements, it constitutes the active core of right-wing socialist parties and poses a serious danger to the working-class movement. This stratum of bourgeois workers is the social basis of opportunism.

Opportunism in the labor movement is the adaptation of the labor movement to the interests of the bourgeoisie by undermining the revolutionary struggle of the proletariat for liberation from capitalist slavery. The opportunists poison the consciousness of the workers by preaching the reformist way of "improving" capitalism, they demand from the workers the support of the bourgeois governments in all their domestic and foreign imperialist policies.

The opportunists are bourgeois agents in the labor movement. By splitting the ranks of the working class, the opportunists prevent the workers from joining forces to overthrow capitalism. This is one of the most important reasons why the bourgeoisie is still in power in many countries.

Pre-monopoly capitalism, with its free competition, was matched by limited bourgeois democracy. Imperialism, with its domination of monopolies, is characterized by a turn from democracy to political reaction in the domestic and foreign policy of the bourgeois states. Political reaction along the whole line is a property of imperialism. The leaders of the monopolies or their henchmen occupy the most important posts in the governments and in the entire state apparatus. Under imperialism, governments are not set up by the people, but by the magnates of finance capital.

The reactionary monopoly cliques, in order to consolidate their power, seek to nullify the democratic rights of the working people won by the stubborn struggle of many generations. This makes it necessary to intensify in every possible way the struggle of the masses for democracy, against imperialism and reaction. "Capitalism in general and imperialism in particular turns democracy into an illusion – and at the same time, capitalism gives rise to democratic aspirations among the masses, creates democratic institutions, sharpens the antagonism between imperialism that denies democracy and the masses striving for democracy"[3].

In the epoch of imperialism, the struggle of the broad masses of the people, led by the working class, against the reaction engendered by the monopolies is of great historical significance. It is precisely on the activity, organization, and determination of the masses that the misanthropic plans of the aggressive forces of imperialism depend, which are constantly preparing new hard trials and military catastrophes.

Imperialism is the eve of the socialist revolution.

Imperialism is dying capitalism. The action of the basic economic law of modern capitalism sharpens all the contradictions of capitalism, brings them to the last line, to the extreme limits beyond which the revolution begins. The most important of these contradictions are the following three contradictions.

First, *the contradiction between labor and capital.* The domination of the monopolies and the financial oligarchy in the capitalist countries leads to intensified exploitation of the working classes. The sharp deterioration in the material situation and the intensification of the political oppression of the working class cause the growth of its indignation and lead to an intensification of the class struggle between the proletariat and the bourgeoisie. Under these conditions, the former methods of the economic and parliamentary struggle of the working class turn out to be completely inadequate. Imperialism is leading the working class to the socialist revolution as the only salvation.

Secondly, *the contradiction between the imperialist powers.* In the struggle for maximum profits, the monopolies of various countries clash, and each of the groups of capitalists seeks to secure predominance for itself by capturing sales markets, sources of raw materials, and spheres of investment of capital. The bitter struggle among the imperialist countries for spheres of influence inevitably leads to imperialist wars, which weaken the position of capitalism in general and advance the socialist revolution.

Thirdly, *the contradiction between the oppressed peoples of the colonies and dependent countries and the imperialist powers that exploit them.* As a result of the development of capitalism in the colonies and semi-colonies, the national liberation movement against imperialism is intensifying. The colonies and dependent countries are being transformed from reserves of imperialism into reserves of the proletarian revolution.

These main contradictions characterize imperialism as dying capitalism. This does not mean that capitalism can die out on its own, in the order of "automatic collapse", without the most resolute struggle of the popular masses, led by the working class, to abolish the rule of the bourgeoisie. It only means that imperialism is that stage in the development of capitalism at which the proletarian revolution has become a practical inevitability and favorable conditions have ripened for a direct assault on the strongholds of capitalism. Therefore, Lenin characterized imperialism as the eve of the socialist revolution.

State monopoly capitalism.

In the era of imperialism, the bourgeois state, representing the dictatorship of the financial oligarchy, carries out all its activities in the interests of the ruling monopolies.

As the contradictions of imperialism sharpen, the ruling monopolies strengthen their direct leadership of the state apparatus. Increasingly, the largest magnates of capital are personally acting as heads of the state apparatus. There is a process of transformation of monopoly capitalism into state-monopoly capitalism. Already the First World War accelerated and intensified this process tremendously.

State-monopoly capitalism consists in subordinating the state apparatus to capitalist monopolies and using it to interfere in the country's economy (especially in connection with its militarization) in order to ensure maximum profits for the monopolies and strengthen the omnipotence of finance capital. At the same time, individual enterprises, industries, and economic functions are transferred into the hands of the state (providing a workforce, supplying scarce raw materials, a rationing system for distributing products, building military enterprises, financing the militarization of the economy, etc.) while maintaining the dominance of private ownership of the means of production in the country.

The monopolies use state power to actively promote the concentration and centralization of capital, to increase the power and influence of the largest monopolies: the state, by special measures, compels independent entrepreneurs to submit to monopoly associations, and in time of war it carries out a forced concentration of production, closing many small and medium-sized enterprises. In the interests of the monopolies, the state, on the one hand, establishes high customs duties on imported goods, and on the other hand, encourages the export of goods by paying export duties to the monopolies and making it easier for them to conquer new markets through dumping.

The monopolies use the state budget to rob the population of their country through taxes and receive orders from the state that bring huge profits. The bourgeois state, under the pretext of "encouraging economic initiative," pays huge sums of money to the largest entrepreneurs in the form of subsidies. If the monopolies are threatened with bankruptcy, they receive funds from the state to cover their losses, and their tax debts to the state are written off.

The development of state-monopoly capitalism is particularly enhanced during the period of preparation and conduct of imperialist wars. Lenin called state-monopoly capitalism hard labor for the workers, a paradise for the capitalists. The governments of the imperialist countries give huge orders to the monopolies for the supply of armaments, equipment, and foodstuffs, build military factories at the expense of the treasury and put them at the disposal of the monopolies, and issue war loans. At the same time, the bourgeois states shift all the burdens of war onto the working people. All this provides the monopolies with enormous profits.

The development of state-monopoly capitalism leads, firstly, to a further acceleration of the capitalist socialization of production, which creates the material preconditions for the replacement of capitalism by socialism. Lenin pointed out that state-monopoly capitalism is the most complete material preparation for socialism.

The development of state-monopoly capitalism leads, secondly, to the intensification of the relative and absolute impoverishment of the proletariat. With the help of state power, the monopolies in every possible way increase the degree of exploitation of the working class, the peasantry, and broad sections of the intelligentsia, which inevitably causes a sharp aggravation of the contradictions between the exploited and the exploiters, and intensifies the struggle of the proletariat and other sections of the working people for the abolition of capitalism.

The defenders of capitalism, concealing the subordination of the bourgeois state to the capitalist monopolies, assert that the state has become the decisive force in the economy of the capitalist countries and is capable of ensuring planned management of the national economy. In reality, however, the bourgeois state cannot manage the economy in a planned manner, since the economy is not at its disposal, but in the hands of the monopolies. All attempts at state "regulation" of the economy under capitalism are powerless in the face of the spontaneous laws of economic life.

The law of uneven economic and political development of the capitalist countries in the period of imperialism and the possibility of the victory of socialism in one country.

Under capitalism, individual enterprises and branches of the country's economy cannot develop evenly. In conditions of competition and anarchy of production, uneven development of the capitalist economy is inevitable. But in the pre-monopoly era, capitalism as a whole was still on the rise. Production was fragmented among a large number of enterprises, free competition reigned, there were no monopolies. Capitalism could still develop relatively smoothly. Some countries outperformed others for a long period of time. On the globe then there were vast, unoccupied territories. The case did without military clashes on a global scale.

The situation changed radically with the transition to monopoly capitalism. The high level of technological development opened up the opportunity for young countries to quickly, in leaps and bounds, overtake and outstrip older rivals. Countries that have embarked on the path of capitalist development later than others use the ready-made results of technical progress - machines, methods of production, etc.

On the other hand, in old countries earlier than in young ones, the domination of monopolies has developed, which are characterized by a tendency to parasitism, decay, stagnation of technology. Hence the fast, abrupt development of some countries, growth retardation of others. This spasmodic development is also greatly intensified by the export of capital. An opportunity is being created for some countries to overtake other countries, to force them out of the markets, to achieve a redistribution of the already divided world with an armed hand. During the period of imperialism, the uneven development of the capitalist countries became the decisive force in imperialist development.

The correlation of the economic forces of the imperialist powers is changing with unprecedented rapidity. The growth of the military forces of the imperialist states is also uneven. The changed balance of economic and military forces inevitably clashes with the old distribution of colonies and spheres of influence. A struggle for the redistribution of the already divided world is brewing. The real might of one imperialist group or another is tested by means of bloody and devastating wars.

In 1860, England occupied the first place in world industrial production; France followed suit. Germany and the United States of America were just emerging on the world stage. A decade has passed, and the rapidly growing country of young capitalism - the United States of America - has overtaken France and switched places with it. A decade later, the United States of America overtook England and firmly took first place in world industrial production, and Germany overtook France and took third place after the USA and England. By the beginning of the 20th century, Germany had pushed aside England, taking second place after the United States. As a result of changes in the correlation of forces among the capitalist countries, the capitalist world splits into two hostile imperialist camps and world wars arise.

Due to the uneven development of the capitalist countries during the period of imperialism, world capitalism cannot develop otherwise than through crises and military catastrophes. The aggravation of contradictions in the camp of imperialism and the inevitability of military clashes lead to the mutual weakening of the imperialists. The world front of imperialism becomes easily vulnerable to the proletarian revolution. On this basis, a breakthrough of the front can take place at the link where the chain of the imperialist front is weakest, at the point where the most favorable conditions for the victory of the proletariat are formed.

The unevenness of economic development in the era of imperialism also determines the unevenness of political development, which means that the political prerequisites for the victory of the proletarian revolution in different countries mature at different times. These prerequisites include, above all, the sharpness of class contradictions and the degree of development of the class struggle, the level of class consciousness, political organization and revolutionary determination of the proletariat, its ability to lead the bulk of the peasantry.

The law of the uneven economic and political development of the capitalist countries during the period of imperialism constitutes the starting point of Lenin's teaching on the possibility of the victory of socialism initially in several countries or even in one country taken separately.

Marx and Engels in the middle of the 19th century, studying pre-monopoly capitalism, came to the conclusion that the socialist revolution can win only simultaneously in all or most of the civilized countries. However, at the beginning of the 20th century, especially during the First World War, the situation changed radically. Pre-monopoly capitalism has grown into monopoly capitalism. Ascending capitalism has turned into descending, dying capitalism. The war exposed the incurable weaknesses of the world imperialist front. At the same time, the law of uneven development predetermined the different timing of the maturation of the proletarian revolution in different countries. Proceeding from the law of the uneven development of capitalism in the era of imperialism, Lenin came to the conclusion that the old formula of Marx and Engels no longer corresponds to the new historical conditions,

"The unevenness of economic and political development," wrote Lenin, "is the unconditional law of capitalism. It follows from this that the victory of socialism is possible initially in a few or even in one, taken separately, capitalist country ."

This was a new, complete theory of the socialist revolution created by Lenin. It enriched Marxism and moved it forward, opened up a revolutionary perspective to the proletarians of individual countries, unleashed the initiative in attacking their own bourgeoisie, strengthened their faith in the victory of the proletarian revolution.

During the period of imperialism, the formation of the capitalist system of the world economy is completed, in connection with which individual countries have become links in a single chain.

Leninism teaches that under conditions of imperialism the socialist revolution first wins not necessarily in those countries where capitalism is most developed and the proletariat constitutes the majority of the population, but above all in those countries which are a weak link in the chain of world imperialism. The objective conditions for a socialist revolution have matured in the entire system of the world capitalist economy. Under such conditions, the presence in this system of countries that are insufficiently developed industrially cannot serve as an obstacle to revolution. The victory of the socialist revolution requires the presence of a revolutionary proletariat and a proletarian vanguard united in a political party,

In the era of imperialism, when the revolutionary movement is growing all over the world, the imperialist bourgeoisie enters into alliance with all reactionary forces without exception and makes every possible use of the survivals of serfdom to increase profits. Because of this, the liquidation of the feudal-serf system is impossible without a determined struggle against imperialism. Under these conditions, the proletariat becomes the hegemon of the bourgeois-democratic revolution, rallying the masses of the peasantry around itself to fight against serfdom and imperialist colonial oppression. As the anti-feudal and national liberation tasks are solved, the bourgeois-democratic revolution develops into a socialist revolution.

During the period of imperialism, the indignation of the proletariat grows in the capitalist countries, elements of a revolutionary explosion accumulate, and a liberation war against imperialism develops in the colonial and dependent countries. Imperialist wars for the redivision of the world weaken the system of imperialism and intensify the tendency to unite the proletarian revolutions in the capitalist countries with the national liberation movement in the colonies.

The proletarian revolution, victorious in one country, is at the same time the beginning of the world socialist revolution and a powerful base for its further development. Lenin scientifically foresaw that the world revolution would develop through the revolutionary falling away of a number of new countries from the system of imperialism with the support given to the proletarians of these countries by the proletariat of the imperialist states. The very process of falling away from imperialism in a number of new countries will proceed the faster and more thoroughly, the more thoroughly socialism is strengthened in the first country of the victorious proletarian revolution.

"The outcome of the struggle," Lenin wrote in 1923, "depends, in the final analysis, on the fact that Russia, India, China, etc. constitute the vast majority of the population. And it is precisely this majority of the population that has been drawn with extraordinary rapidity in recent years into the struggle for its liberation, so that in this sense there can be no shadow of doubt as to what the final solution of the world struggle will be.

In this sense, the final victory of socialism is completely and unconditionally assured" [5] .

SUMMARY
1. Imperialism is a special and final stage of capitalism. Imperialism is: 1) monopoly capitalism, 2) decaying or parasitic capitalism, 3) dying capitalism, on the eve of the socialist revolution.

2. The decay and parasitism of capitalism is expressed in the retardation by the monopolies of technical progress and the growth of productive forces, in the transformation of a number of bourgeois countries into rentier states living off the exploitation of the peoples of the colonies and dependent countries, in rampant militarism, in the growth of the parasitic consumption of the bourgeoisie, in a reactionary domestic and the foreign policy of the imperialist states, in the bribery of the bourgeoisie of the imperialist countries of the small top of the working class. The decay of capitalism sharply increases the impoverishment of the working class and the working masses of the peasantry.

3. As a result of the operation of the basic economic law of modern capitalism, the three main contradictions of imperialism are sharply exacerbated: 1) the contradiction between labor and capital, 2) the contradiction between the imperialist powers fighting for predominance, in the final analysis, for world domination, and 3) the contradiction between metropolises and colonies. Imperialism is bringing the proletariat close to the socialist revolution.

4. State-monopoly capitalism is the subordination of the state apparatus to capitalist monopolies in order to ensure maximum profits and strengthen the dominance of the financial oligarchy. Meaning the highest stage of the capitalist socialization of production, state-monopoly capitalism brings with it a further intensification of the exploitation of the working class, the impoverishment and ruin of the broad working masses.

5. The law of uneven economic and political development of the capitalist countries during the period of imperialism weakens the united front of world imperialism. The uneven maturation of the revolution excludes the possibility of a simultaneous victory of socialism in all countries or in most countries. It creates the possibility of breaking through the imperialist chain at its weakest link, the possibility of the victory of the socialist revolution initially in a few or even in one country taken separately.

[1] V. I. Lenin, Imperialism and the split of socialism, Works, vol. 23, p. 94.
[2] V. I. Lenin, Civilized barbarism, Works, vol. 19, p. 349.
[3] V. I. Lenin, Works, vol. 23, p. 13.
[4] V. I. Lenin, On the slogan of the United States of Europe, Works, vol. 21, p. 311.
[5] V. I. Lenin, Better less, but better, Works, vol. 33, p. 458.

The essence of the general crisis of capitalism.

Along with the growth of the contradictions of imperialism, the prerequisites for a general crisis of capitalism were accumulating. The extreme aggravation of the contradictions in the camp of imperialism, the clashes of the imperialist powers, resulting in world wars, the combination of the class struggle of the proletariat in the mother countries and the national liberation struggle of the peoples in the colonies - all this leads to a sharp weakening of the world capitalist system, to breaking the chain of imperialism and the revolutionary falling away of individual countries. from the capitalist system. The foundations of the doctrine of the general crisis of capitalism were developed by V. I. Lenin.

The general crisis of capitalism is an all-round crisis of the world capitalist system as a whole, characterized by wars and revolutions, the struggle between dying capitalism and growing socialism. The general crisis of capitalism embraces all aspects of capitalism, both economics and politics. It is based on the ever-increasing disintegration of the world economic system of capitalism, on the one hand, and the growing economic power of the countries that have fallen away from capitalism, on the other.

The fundamental features of the general crisis of capitalism are: the split of the world into two systems - capitalist and socialist - and the struggle between them, the crisis of the colonial system of imperialism, the aggravation of the problem of markets and the emergence in connection with this of chronic underloading of enterprises and chronic mass unemployment.

The uneven development of the capitalist countries in the epoch of imperialism in the course of time gives rise to a discrepancy between the existing division of sales markets, spheres of influence and colonies and the changed correlation of forces of the main capitalist states. On this basis, a sharp imbalance arises within the world system of capitalism, leading to a split of the capitalist world into hostile groups, to a war between them. World wars weaken the forces of imperialism and facilitate the breakthrough of the imperialist front and the falling away of individual countries from the capitalist system.

The general crisis of capitalism covers a whole historical period, which is an integral part of the era of imperialism. As has already been pointed out, the law of the uneven economic and political development of the capitalist countries in the era of imperialism predetermines the difference in timing of the maturation of the socialist revolution in different countries. Lenin pointed out that the general crisis of capitalism is not a simultaneous act, but a long period of turbulent economic and political upheavals, an intensified class struggle, a period of "the collapse of capitalism in all its scale and the birth of a socialist society" [1] . This determines the historical inevitability of the long coexistence of the two systems - socialist and capitalist.

The general crisis of capitalism began during the First World War and unfolded especially as a result of the fall of the Soviet Union from the capitalist system. This was the first stage of the general crisis of capitalism. During the Second World War, the second stage of the general crisis of capitalism unfolded, especially after the people's democracies in Europe and Asia fell away from the capitalist system.

World War I and the beginning of the general crisis of capitalism.

The First World War was the result of the aggravation of contradictions between the imperialist powers on the basis of the struggle for the redivision of the world and spheres of influence. Next to the old imperialist powers, new predators have grown up, late to the division of the world. German imperialism entered the scene. Germany, later than a number of other countries, embarked on the path of capitalist development and came to the division of markets and spheres of influence, when the world was divided among the old imperialist powers.

However, by the beginning of the 20th century, Germany, having overtaken England in terms of industrial development, took second place in the world and first in Europe. Germany began to push England and France on the world markets. The change in the correlation of the economic and military forces of the main capitalist states raised the question of the redistribution of the world. In the struggle for the redivision of the world, Germany, acting in alliance with Austria-Hungary and Italy, faced England, France, and Tsarist Russia dependent on them.

Germany sought to take away part of the colonies from England and France, to oust England from the Middle East and put an end to its maritime dominance, to take Ukraine, Poland, the Baltic States from Russia, to subjugate all of Central and South-Eastern Europe. In turn, England sought to put an end to German competition in the world market and fully consolidate dominance in the Middle East and the African continent. France set the task - to return the conquered by Germany in 1870 - 1871. Alsace and Lorraine and seize the Saar Basin from Germany. Tsarist Russia and other bourgeois states that participated in the war also pursued predatory goals.

The struggle of two imperialist blocs - Anglo-French and German - for the redivision of the world affected the interests of all imperialist countries and therefore led to a world war, in which Japan, the USA and a number of other countries later took part. The First World War had an imperialist character on both sides.

The war shook the capitalist world to its deepest foundations. In its scale, it left far behind all previous wars in the history of mankind.

The war was a source of enormous enrichment for the monopolies. The US capitalists have especially profited. The profits of all American monopolies in 1917 exceeded the level of profits in 1914 by three or four times. During the five years of the war (from 1914 to 1918), the American monopolies received over 35 billion dollars in profit (before taxes). The largest monopolies have increased their profits tenfold.

The population of the countries that actively participated in the war was about 800 million people. About 70 million people were drafted into the army. The war has consumed as many human lives as have died in all the wars in Europe in a thousand years. The number of those killed reached 10 million, the number of wounded and maimed exceeded 20 million. Millions of people died from hunger and epidemics. The war brought colossal damage to the national economy of the warring countries. During the entire war (1914-1918), the direct military expenditures of the belligerent powers amounted to $208 billion (in the prices of the corresponding years).

During the war, the significance of the monopolies grew, and their subordination to the state apparatus increased. The state apparatus was used by the largest monopolies to ensure maximum profits. Military "regulation" of the economy was carried out in order to enrich the largest monopolies. To this end, in a number of countries the working day was extended, strikes were banned, barracks were introduced and forced labor was introduced at enterprises. The main source of unprecedented growth in profits was government military orders at the expense of the budget.

During the war, military expenditures absorbed a huge part of the national income and were covered primarily by increasing taxes on the working people. The main part of the military appropriations went to the monopolists in the form of payment for military orders, irrevocable loans, and subsidies. Prices for military orders ensured huge profits for the monopolies. Lenin called military supplies legitimized embezzlement. The monopolies profited by reducing the real wages of workers through inflation, as well as by direct robbery of the occupied territories.

During the war, a rationing system for food distribution was introduced in European countries, which limited the consumption of workers to starvation rations.

The war brought the poverty and suffering of the masses to the extreme, it aggravated class contradictions and provoked an upsurge in the revolutionary struggle of the working class and working peasants in the capitalist countries. At the same time, the war, which had turned from a European into a world war, drew the colonies and dependent countries into its orbit and rear of imperialism, which facilitated the union of the revolutionary movement in Europe with the national liberation movement of the peoples of the East.

The war weakened world capitalism. "The European war," Lenin wrote then, "means the greatest historical crisis, the beginning of a new era. Like any crisis, the war exacerbated deep-seated contradictions and brought them out . It gave rise to a mighty upsurge in the anti-imperialist revolutionary movement.

The victory of the Great October Socialist Revolution and the split of the world into two systems: capitalist and socialist.

The proletarian revolution broke through the front of imperialism first of all in Russia, which turned out to be the weakest link in the chain of imperialism. Russia was the focal point of all the contradictions of imperialism. In Russia, the omnipotence of capital was intertwined with tsarist despotism, with the remnants of serfdom and colonial oppression of non-Russian peoples. Lenin called tsarism "military-feudal imperialism".

Tsarist Russia was a reserve of Western imperialism as a sphere of application for foreign capital, which held in its hands the decisive branches of industry - fuel and metallurgy, and as a pillar of Western imperialism in the East, connecting the financial capital of the West with the colonies of the East. The interests of tsarism and Western imperialism merged into a single tangle of imperialist interests.

The high concentration of Russian industry and the presence of such a revolutionary party as the Communist Party have made the working class of Russia the greatest force in the political life of the country. The Russian proletariat had such a serious ally as the peasant poor, who constituted the vast majority of the peasant population. Under these conditions, the bourgeois-democratic revolution in Russia was bound to grow into a socialist revolution, take on an international character and shake the very foundations of world imperialism.

The international significance of the Great October Socialist Revolution lies in the fact that, firstly, it broke through the front of imperialism, overthrew the imperialist bourgeoisie in one of the largest capitalist countries, and for the first time in history placed the proletariat in power; secondly, it not only undermined imperialism in the mother countries, but also struck at the rear of imperialism, undermining its rule in the colonies and dependent countries; thirdly, by weakening the power of imperialism in the mother countries and undermining its dominance in the colonies, it thereby called into question the very existence of world imperialism as a whole.

The Great October Socialist Revolution meant a radical turn in the world history of mankind; it ushered in a new era—the era of proletarian revolutions in the imperialist countries and the national liberation movement in the colonies. The October Revolution wrested one-sixth of the land from the power of capital of the working people, which meant the split of the world into two systems: capitalist and socialist. The split of the world into two systems was the most striking expression of the general crisis of capitalism. As a result of the split of the world into two systems, a fundamentally new contradiction of world-historical significance arose - the contradiction between dying capitalism and growing socialism. The struggle between the two systems - capitalism and socialism - has acquired decisive importance in the modern era.

Describing the general crisis of capitalism, J.V. Stalin said:

> "This means, first of all, that the imperialist war and its consequences have intensified the decay of capitalism and undermined its balance, that we now live in an era of wars and revolutions, that capitalism is no longer the only and the entire embracing system of the world economy, that along with the capitalist economic system there is a socialist system which is growing, which is prospering, which opposes the capitalist system and which, by the very fact of its existence, demonstrates the rottenness of capitalism, shakes its foundations" [3] .

The first years after the war 1914-1918 were a period of acute disruption in the economy of the capitalist countries, a period of fierce struggle between the proletariat and the bourgeoisie.

As a result of the shock of world capitalism and under the direct influence of the Great October Socialist Revolution, a number of revolutions and revolutionary uprisings took place both on the European continent and in colonial and semi-colonial countries. This powerful revolutionary movement, the sympathy and support given to Soviet Russia by the working masses of the whole world, predetermined the collapse of all attempts by world imperialism to strangle the world's first socialist republic. In 1920 - 1921 the main capitalist countries were gripped by a deep economic crisis.

Having emerged from the post-war economic chaos, the capitalist world entered a period of relative stabilization in 1924. The revolutionary upsurge gave way to a temporary ebb of revolution in a number of European countries. It was a temporary, partial stabilization of capitalism, achieved through increased exploitation of the working people. Under the flag of capitalist "rationalization" a brutal intensification of labor was carried out. Capitalist stabilization inevitably led to an aggravation of contradictions between workers and capitalists, between imperialism and the colonial peoples, and between the imperialists of different countries. The world economic crisis that began in 1929 put an end to capitalist stabilization.

At the same time, the national economy of the USSR developed steadily along an ascending line, without crises or catastrophes. The Soviet Union was then the only country that did not know the crises and other contradictions of capitalism. The industry of the Soviet Union went up all the time at a pace unprecedented in history. In 1938, the industrial output of the USSR was 908.8% compared with the output of 1913, while the industrial output of the USA was only 120%, England - 113.3, France - 93.2%. A comparison of the economic development of the USSR and the capitalist countries clearly reveals the decisive advantages of the socialist economic system and the doom of the capitalist system.

The experience of the USSR has shown that the working people can successfully manage the country, build, and manage the economy without the bourgeoisie and against the bourgeoisie. Every year of peaceful competition between socialism and capitalism undermines and weakens capitalism and strengthens socialism.

The emergence of the world's first socialist state introduced a new moment in the development of the revolutionary struggle of the working people. The USSR is a powerful center of attraction around which the united front of the peoples' revolutionary and national liberation struggle against imperialism is rallying. International imperialism seeks to stifle or at least weaken the socialist state. The camp of imperialism is trying to resolve its internal difficulties and contradictions by fomenting war against the USSR. In the struggle against the intrigues of imperialism, the Soviet Union relies on its economic and military might, on the support of the international proletariat.

Historical experience has shown that in the struggle between the two systems, the socialist economic system is assured of victory over capitalism on the basis of peaceful competition. The Soviet state in its foreign policy proceeds from the possibility of the peaceful coexistence of the two systems—capitalism and socialism—and firmly adheres to the policy of peace among peoples.

The crisis of the colonial system of imperialism.

An integral part of the general crisis of capitalism is the crisis of the colonial system of imperialism. Having arisen during the

First World War, this crisis is expanding and deepening. The crisis of the colonial system of imperialism consists in a sharp aggravation of the contradictions between the imperialist powers, on the one hand, and the colonies and dependent countries, on the other, in the development of the national liberation struggle of the oppressed peoples of these countries, headed by the industrial proletariat.

During the period of the general crisis of capitalism, the role of the colonies as a source of maximum profits for the monopolies increases. The intensification of the struggle between the imperialists for markets and spheres of influence, the aggravation of internal difficulties and contradictions in the capitalist countries, lead to increased pressure on the colonies by the imperialists and to an increase in the exploitation of the peoples of the colonial and dependent countries.

The First World War, during which the export of industrial goods from the metropolises sharply decreased, gave a significant impetus to the industrial development of the colonies. In the period between the two wars, as a result of the intensified export of capital to backward countries, capitalism continued to develop in the colonies. In this regard, the proletariat grew in the colonial countries.

The total number of industrial enterprises in India grew from 2,874 in 1914 to 10,466 in 1939. In connection with this, the number of factory workers increased. The number of workers in the Indian manufacturing industry in 1914 was 951 thousand people, and in 1939 - 1,751.1 thousand people. The total number of workers in India, including miners, railway and water transport workers, and plantation workers, in 1939 was about 5 million people. In China (without Manchuria), the number of industrial enterprises (with at least 30 workers) grew from 200 in 1910 to 2,500 in 1937, and the number of workers employed in them increased from 150,000 people in 1910 to 2,750,000. man in 1937 Taking into account the more industrially developed Manchuria, the number of workers in industry and transport (not counting small enterprises) in China on the eve of the Second World War was about 4 million people. The industrial proletariat has grown considerably in Indonesia, Malaya, African and other colonies.

During the period of the general crisis of capitalism, the exploitation of the working class of the colonies intensifies. The commission, which examined the situation of Indian workers in 1929-1931, found that the family of an ordinary worker has an income per family member that is only about half the cost of maintaining a prisoner in Bombay prisons. The bulk of the workers fall into enslaving debt dependence on usurers. Forced labor became widespread in the colonies, especially in the mining industry and agriculture (on plantations).

The growth of the working class in the colonial countries and the intensification of the national liberation struggle of the peoples of these countries radically undermine the positions of imperialism and signify a new stage in the development of the national liberation movement in the colonies. Lenin taught that after the victory of the Great October Socialist Revolution, which broke through the front of world imperialism, a new era of colonial revolutions opened. If earlier the national liberation struggle ended with the establishment of the power of the bourgeoisie and thereby cleared the way for the freer development of capitalism, now, in the era of the general crisis of capitalism, the national-colonial revolutions, carried out under the leadership of the proletariat, lead to the establishment of people's power, ensuring the development of the country according to way to socialism, bypassing the capitalist stage of development.

As has been pointed out, despite some development of industry, imperialism hinders the economic development of the colonies. As before, heavy industry is not being developed in these countries, and they remain agricultural and raw material appendages to the metropolises. Imperialism preserves the remnants of feudal relations that exist in the colonies, using them to intensify the exploitation of the oppressed peoples. Moreover, the well-known development of capitalist relations in the countryside, which destroys natural forms of economy, only intensifies the degree of exploitation and pauperization of the peasantry. The struggle against the survivals of feudalism is the basis of the bourgeois-democratic revolution in the colonial countries.

The bourgeois-democratic revolution in the colonies is directed not only against feudal oppression, but at the same time against imperialism. It is impossible to abolish feudal survivals in the colonies without the revolutionary overthrow of imperialist oppression. The colonial revolution is the union of two streams of revolutionary movement—the movement against feudal survivals and the movement against imperialism. In this regard, the largest force in the colonial revolutions is the peasantry, which constitutes the bulk of the population of the colonies.

The working class becomes the hegemon (leader) of the revolution in the colonies, being a consistent fighter against imperialism, able to rally the many millions of peasants and carry the revolution to the end. The alliance of the working class and the peasantry under the leadership of the working class is the decisive condition for the success of the national liberation struggle of the oppressed peoples of the colonial countries.

A certain section of the local bourgeoisie, the so-called comprador bourgeoisie, which acts as an intermediary between foreign capital and the local market, is a direct agent of foreign imperialism. As for the national bourgeoisie in the colonies, whose interests are infringed upon by foreign capital, at a certain stage of the revolution they can support the struggle against imperialism. However, the national bourgeoisie in the colonies is weak and inconsistent in the struggle against imperialism.

The Great October Socialist Revolution unleashed a whole series of powerful national liberation movements in China, Indonesia, India, and other countries. It opened a new era - the era of colonial revolutions, in which the leadership belongs to the proletariat.

Aggravation of the problem of markets, chronic underutilization of enterprises and chronic mass unemployment.

An integral feature of the general crisis of capitalism is the progressive aggravation of the problem of markets and the resulting chronic underutilization of enterprises and chronic mass unemployment.

The aggravation of the problem of markets during the period of the general crisis of capitalism is caused primarily by the dropping out of individual countries from the world system of imperialism. Russia's falling away from the capitalist system, with its huge sales markets and sources of raw materials, could not but affect the economic situation of the capitalist world. The action of the basic economic law of modern capitalism is inevitably accompanied by the growing impoverishment of the working people, whose standard of living is kept by the capitalists at an extreme minimum, which leads to an aggravation of the problem of markets. The aggravation of the problem of markets is also caused by the development in the colonies and dependent countries of their own capitalism, which successfully competes in the markets with the old capitalist countries.

As a result, instead of a growing market, as it was before, the period between the two world wars created a relative stability of markets with the growth of the production possibilities of capitalism. This could not but aggravate all capitalist contradictions to the extreme. "This contradiction between the growth of productive possibilities and the relative stability of markets underlies the fact that the problem of markets is now the main problem of capitalism. The aggravation of the problem of sales markets in general, the aggravation of the problem of foreign markets in particular, the aggravation of the problem of markets for the export of capital in particular - such is the present state of capitalism.

This, in fact, explains why underloading of plants and factories is becoming a common phenomenon" [4] . Previously, mass underloading of factories and factories took place only during economic crises. The period of the general crisis of capitalism is characterized by a chronic underutilization of enterprises.

So, during the period of the rise of 1925 - 1929. The production capacity of the manufacturing industry in the United States was used only by 80%. In 1930 - 1934 the utilization of the production capacity of the manufacturing industry has decreased to 60%. At the same time, it must be taken into account that the US bourgeois statistics, when calculating the production capacity of the manufacturing industry, did not take into account long-term inactive enterprises and accepted as a condition the work of enterprises in one shift.

In close connection with the chronic underutilization of enterprises is chronic mass unemployment. Before the First World War, the reserve army of labor grew during the years of crises, and during periods of upsurge it was reduced to a relatively small size. During the period of the general crisis of capitalism, unemployment acquires enormous proportions and remains at a high level even in years of recovery and expansion. The reserve army of labor has become a permanent army of millions of unemployed.

At the moment of the highest rise in industry between the two world wars - in 1929 - the number of completely unemployed in the USA was about 2 million people, and in subsequent years, until the Second World War, it did not fall below 8 million people. In England, the number of completely unemployed among the insured did not drop from 1922 to 1938 below 1.2 million people a year. Millions of workers made their living by casual work, suffered from partial unemployment.

Chronic mass unemployment sharply worsens the position of the working class. Long-term unemployment is becoming the main form of unemployment. The presence of chronic mass unemployment makes it possible for the capitalists to enormously increase the intensity of labor in enterprises, to throw out workers already exhausted by excessive work and to recruit new, stronger, and healthier ones. In this regard, the "working age" of the worker and the duration of his work at the enterprise are greatly reduced. Increasing uncertainty of employed workers in the future. Capitalists use chronic mass unemployment to drastically reduce the wages of employed workers. The income of a working family is also declining due to a decrease in the number of working family members.

In the USA, according to bourgeois statistics, the rise in unemployment from 1920 to 1933 was accompanied by a fall in the average annual wages of workers employed in industry, construction, and railroad transport, from $1,483 in 1920 to $915 in 1933, i.e. by 38.3%. Unemployed family members are forced to support their existence at the expense of the meager wages of working family members. If the entire wage fund is attributed not only to the employed, but to all workers, both employed and unemployed, then it turns out that earnings per worker (including the unemployed) have decreased due to the increase in unemployment from $1,332 to 1920 to $497 in 1933, i.e. by 62.7%.

Chronic mass unemployment has a serious impact on the position of the peasantry. First, it narrows the domestic market and reduces the demand of the urban population for agricultural products. This leads to deepening agrarian crises.

Secondly, it worsens the situation on the labor market and makes it difficult to involve in industrial production the peasants who are ruined and flee to the cities in search of work. As a result, agrarian overpopulation, and the pauperization of the peasantry increase. Chronic mass unemployment, like chronic underutilization of enterprises, is evidence of the progressive decay of capitalism, its inability to use the productive forces of society.

The intensified exploitation of the working class and the sharp decline in its standard of living during the period of the general crisis of capitalism lead to a further aggravation of the contradictions between labor and capital.

Deepening crises of overproduction and changes in the capitalist cycle.

The narrowing of sales markets and the development of mass chronic unemployment, which occur simultaneously with the growth of production possibilities, extremely sharpen the contradictions of capitalism and lead to a deepening crisis of overproduction, to significant changes in the capitalist cycle.

These changes boil down to the following: the duration of the cycle is shortened, as a result of which crises become more frequent; the depth and severity of crises is growing, which finds expression in the intensification of the decline in production, in the growth of unemployment, etc.; the way out of the crisis becomes more difficult, in connection with which the duration of the crisis phase increases, the phase of depression lengthens, and the rise becomes less and less stable and less and less long.

Prior to World War I, economic crises usually occurred every 10 to 12 years, and only occasionally after 8 years. In the period between the two world wars - from 1920 to 1938, that is, in 18 years, there were three economic crises: in 1920 - 1921, in 1929 - 1933, in 1937 - 1938.

The depth of the decline in production increases from crisis to crisis. US manufacturing output fell during the crisis of 1907-1908. (from the highest point before the crisis to the lowest point of the crisis) by 16.4%, during the crisis of 1920-1921. - by 23, and during the crisis of 1929 - 1933. - by 47.1%.

The economic crisis of 1929 - 1933 was the deepest crisis of overproduction. This was the influence of the general crisis of capitalism. "The current crisis," said E. Telman, "has the character of a cyclical crisis within the framework of the general crisis of the capitalist system in the era of monopoly capitalism. Here we must understand the dialectical interplay between the general crisis and the periodic crisis.

On the one hand, the periodic crisis takes on sharp, unprecedented forms, since it proceeds on the basis of the general crisis of capitalism and is determined by the conditions of monopoly capitalism. On the other hand, the destruction caused by the periodic crisis again deepens and accelerates the general crisis of the capitalist system." [5]

The economic crisis of 1929 - 1933 embraced all countries of the capitalist world without exception. As a result, it was impossible for some countries to maneuver at the expense of others. With the greatest force, the crisis hit the largest country of modern capitalism - the United States of America. The industrial crisis in the main capitalist countries intertwined with the agricultural crisis in the agrarian countries, which led to a deepening of the economic crisis as a whole. Crisis of 1929 - 1933 turned out to be the deepest and most acute of all economic crises in the history of capitalism. Industrial production throughout the capitalist world fell by 36%, and in some countries even more. The turnover of world trade has fallen to one third. The finances of the capitalist countries have fallen into complete disorder.

In conditions of chronic mass unemployment, economic crises lead to a huge increase in the number of unemployed.

The percentage of completely unemployed at the time of the greatest decline in production, according to official data, was 32% in the USA in 1932, and 22% in England. In Germany, the percentage of completely unemployed among trade union members in 1932 reached 43.8% and partially unemployed - 22.6%. In absolute figures, the number of completely unemployed in 1932 was: in the USA, according to official figures, 13.2 million people, in Germany, 5.5 million people, and in England, 2.8 million people. In the entire capitalist world in 1933 there were 30 million completely unemployed people. The number of semi-unemployed reached enormous proportions. Thus, in the USA the number of semi-unemployed in February 1932 amounted to 11 million people.

The chronic underutilization of factories and factories and the extreme impoverishment of the masses make it difficult to get out of the crisis. The chronic underutilization of enterprises limits the scope for renewal and expansion of fixed capital and hinders the transition from depression to revival and recovery.

In the same direction, chronic mass unemployment and a policy of high monopoly prices act, limiting the expansion of the sale of consumer goods. As a result, the crisis phase is lengthening. If earlier crises were eliminated in one or two years, then the crisis of 1929-1933. lasted over four years.

The revival and upsurge that followed the crisis of 1920-1921 were very uneven and more than once interrupted by partial crises. In the USA, partial crises of overproduction took place in 1924 and 1927. In England and Germany, a significant drop in production occurred in 1926. After the crisis of 1929-1933. not an ordinary depression, but a special kind of depression, which did not lead to a new upsurge and flourishing of industry, although it did not return it to the point of greatest decline. After a depression of a special kind, there was a certain revival, which, however, did not lead to a flourishing on a new, higher basis. By the middle of 1937, world capitalist industry had risen to only 95-96% of the 1929 level, after which a new economic crisis began, which arose in the United States and then spread to England, France, and a number of other countries.

The volume of industrial output in 1938 compared with the level of 1929 decreased in the USA to 72%, in France - to 70%. The total volume of industrial production in the capitalist world in 1938 was 10.3% lower than in 1937.

Crisis of 1937 - 1938 different from the crisis of 1929-1933. first of all, by the fact that it did not arise after a phase of industrial prosperity, as was the case in 1929, but after a special kind of depression and a certain revival. Further, this crisis began at a time when Japan unleashed a war in China, and Germany and Italy transferred their economy to the rails of a war economy, when all the other capitalist countries began to reorganize themselves on a war footing. This meant that capitalism had far fewer resources for a normal exit from this crisis than during the crisis of 1929-1933.

Under the conditions of the general crisis of capitalism, agrarian crises are becoming more frequent and deepening. Following the agrarian crisis in the first half of the 1920s, a new deep agrarian crisis began in 1928, which lasted until the Second World War. The relative overproduction of agricultural products caused a sharp drop in prices, which worsened the position of the peasantry.

In the United States, in 1921, the price index received by farmers fell to 58.5% of the 1920 level, and in 1932 to 43.6% of the 1928 level. In connection with this, the level of agricultural production and peasant incomes fell. U.S. crop production declined in 1934 to 67.9% of the 1928 level and to 70.6% of the 1920 level.

The ruin and pauperization of the main masses of the peasantry cause the growth of revolutionary sentiments among them and push the peasantry onto the path of struggle against capitalism under the leadership of the working class.

Under the conditions of the general crisis of capitalism, the course of capitalist reproduction and the capitalist cycle are greatly influenced by the arms race and world wars used by the monopolies to ensure maximum profits. At first, military-inflationary factors may lead to a temporary revival of the market situation. Preparations for war can slow down the entry of a capitalist country into an economic crisis.

But wars and the militarization of the economy cannot save the capitalist economy from crises. Moreover, they are the most important factor deepening and exacerbating economic crises. World wars lead to a huge destruction of the productive forces and social wealth: factories and factories, stocks of material values, human lives. Wars, by intensifying the impoverishment of the working people and the uneven and disproportionate development of the capitalist economy, prepare the conditions for new, deeper crises of overproduction.

Similarly, the arms race and preparations for war, while temporarily postponing the onset of the crisis, create the conditions for the onset of the crisis in an even more acute form. The militarization of the economy means expanding the production of weapons and equipment for the army by narrowing the production of means of production and consumer goods, an exorbitant increase in taxes and an increase in high prices, which inevitably leads to a sharp reduction in consumption by the population and prepares for the onset of a new economic crisis.

The intensification of decay during the period of the general crisis of capitalism is reflected in the general decrease in the rate of production. The average annual growth rates of industrial production in the capitalist world were: for the period from 1890 to 1913 - 3.7%, for the period from 1913 to 1929 - 2.4%, and for the period from 1929 to 1938, production did not increase, but decreased.

In the period of the general crisis of capitalism, the monopoly bourgeoisie, striving to delay the collapse of the capitalist system and maintain its dominance, wages a furious attack on the standard of living of the working people and imposes police methods of administration. In all the main capitalist countries the development of state-monopoly capitalism is intensifying.

No longer able to rule by the old methods of parliamentarism and bourgeois democracy, the bourgeoisie in a number of countries—Italy, Germany, Japan, and some others—established fascist regimes. Fascism is an open terrorist dictatorship of the most reactionary and aggressive groups of finance capital. Fascism aims inside the country to smash the organizations of the working class and suppress all progressive forces, and outside it to prepare and launch an aggressive war for world domination. Fascism achieves these aims by methods of terror and social demagogy.

Thus, the global economic crisis of 1929-1933. and the crisis of 1937-1938. led to a particularly sharp aggravation of contradictions both within the capitalist countries and between them. The imperialist states sought a way out of these contradictions by preparing for a war for a new redivision of the world.

SUMMARY

1. The general crisis of capitalism is an all-round crisis of the world capitalist system as a whole. It covers both economics and politics. It is based on the ever-increasing disintegration of the world economic system of capitalism, on the one hand, and the growing economic power of the countries that have fallen away from capitalism, on the other.

2. The general crisis of capitalism covers a whole historical period, the content of which is the collapse of capitalism and the victory of socialism on a world scale. The general crisis of capitalism began during the First World War, and especially as a result of the fall of the Soviet Union from the capitalist system.

3. The Great October Socialist Revolution meant a radical turn in the world history of mankind from the old, capitalist, to the new, socialist, world. The split of the world into two systems - the system of capitalism and the system of socialism - and the struggle between them is the main sign of the general crisis of capitalism. With the split of the world into two systems, two lines of economic development were determined: while the capitalist system is becoming more and more entangled in insoluble contradictions, the socialist system is developing steadily along an ascending line, without crises and catastrophes.

4. An integral part of the general crisis of capitalism is the crisis of the colonial system of imperialism. This crisis consists in the development of the national liberation struggle, which is shaking the foundations of imperialism in the colonies. The working class stands at the head of the national liberation struggle of the oppressed peoples. The Great October Socialist Revolution unleashed the revolutionary activity of the oppressed peoples and ushered in the era of colonial revolutions led by the proletariat.

5. Under the conditions of the general crisis of capitalism, as a result of the falling away from the imperialist system of individual countries, the intensification of the impoverishment of the working people, and also as a result of the development

of capitalism in the colonies, the problem of the market is aggravated. A characteristic feature of the general crisis of capitalism is chronic underutilization of enterprises and chronic mass unemployment. Under the influence of the aggravation of the problem of the market, the chronic underload of enterprises and chronic mass unemployment, economic crises are deepening and significant changes are taking place in the capitalist cycle.

[1] V. I. Lenin, Report on the revision of the program and the change of the name of the party at the VII Congress of the RCP (b), Works, vol. 27, p. 106.

[2] V. I. Lenin, Dead Chauvinism and Living Socialism, Works, vol. 21, p. 81.

[3] J. V. Stalin, Political Report of the Central Committee to the 16th Congress of the All-Union Communist Party of Bolsheviks, Works, vol. 12, p. 246.
[4] I. V. Stalin, Political report of the Central Committee to the XV Congress of the CPSU (b), Works, vol. 10, p. 275.

[5] E. Thalmann, Tasks of the People's Revolution in Germany. Report at the plenum of the Central Committee of the KKE on January 15, 1931, 1931, pp. 27-28.

Economic doctrines of the era of capitalism

With the development of capitalism and the growth of its contradictions, various directions of economic thought took shape and developed, expressing the interests of certain classes.

Bourgeois classical political economy.

In the struggle against feudalism, for the establishment of the capitalist order, the bourgeoisie created its own political economy, which debunked the economic views of the ideologists of feudalism and for a certain time played a progressive role.

The capitalist mode of production established itself primarily in England. Bourgeois classical political economy was also born here. William Petty (1623 - 1687), whose activity dates back to the period of the decay of mercantilism, in an effort to discover the inner connection of the economic phenomena of bourgeois society, made the important discovery that goods are exchanged in accordance with the amount of labor required for their production.

The Physiocrats played an important role in the creation of bourgeois political economy . Francois Quesnay (1694 - 1774) was at the head of this direction . The Physiocrats came out in France in the second half of the 18th century, during the period of ideological preparation for the bourgeois revolution. Like the representatives of the French educational philosophy of that time, the physiocrats believed that there were natural laws of human society given by nature. France was at that time an agricultural country. In contrast to the mercantilists, who saw wealth only in money, the Physiocrats declared nature to be the only source of wealth and, therefore, agriculture, which provides man with the fruits of nature. Hence the name of the school - "Physiocrats", made up of two Greek words meaning: nature and power.

The doctrine of the "pure product" occupied a central place in the theory of the Physiocrats. So the physiocrats called the entire surplus of the product in excess of the costs invested in production - that part of the product in which surplus value is embodied under capitalism. The Physiocrats understood wealth as a definite mass of products in their material, natural form, as a definite mass of use values. They argued that the "pure product" arises exclusively in agriculture and animal husbandry, that is, in those industries where the natural processes of growth of plants and animals occur, while in all other industries the form of products delivered by agriculture only changes.

The most significant work of the physiocratic school was Quesnay 's "economic table" . The merit of Quesnay was that he made a remarkable attempt to present the process of capitalist reproduction as a whole, although he failed to give a scientific theory of reproduction.

Based on the fact that the "pure product" is created only in agriculture, the Physiocrats demanded that all taxes be imposed on landowners, and industrialists should be exempted from tax burdens. This demand made clear the class nature of the physiocrats as the ideologists of the bourgeoisie. The Physiocrats were supporters of the unlimited domination of private property. Arguing that only free competition corresponds to the natural laws of the economy and human nature, they opposed the policy of protectionism to the policy of free trade, fought resolutely against shop restrictions and against state interference in the economic life of the country.

Bourgeois classical political economy reached its highest development in the works of A. Smith and D. Ricardo.

Adam Smith (1723-1790) made a significant step forward in the scientific analysis of the capitalist mode of production compared to the Physiocrats. His principal work is An Inquiry into the Nature and Causes of the Wealth of Nations (1776). The wealth of a country lies, according to Smith, in the whole mass of goods produced in it. He rejected the one-sided and therefore incorrect notion of the Physiocrats that the "pure product" is created only by agricultural labor, and for the first time proclaimed any labor as a source of value, in whatever branch of production it was spent. Smith was an economist of the manufacturing period of the development of capitalism, so he saw the basis for increasing labor productivity in the division of labor.

Smith was characterized by the interweaving of two different approaches to economic phenomena. On the one hand, Smith explores the inner connection of phenomena, trying to penetrate his analysis into the hidden structure or, in Marx's words, into the physiology of the bourgeois economic system. On the other hand, Smith gives a description of phenomena as they appear on the surface of capitalist society and, therefore, as they appear to the practical capitalist. The first of these ways of understanding is scientific, the second is non-scientific.

Exploring the internal connection of the phenomena of capitalism, Smith determined the value of a commodity by the amount of labor expended on its production; at the same time, he considered the wages of the wage worker as part of the product of his labor, determined by the value of the means of subsistence, and profit and rent as a deduction from the product created by the labor of the worker. However, Smith did not consistently pursue this view. Smith constantly confused the determination of the value of commodities by the labor contained in them with the determination of the value of commodities by the "value of labour." He argued that the determination of value by labor only referred to the "primitive state of society", by which he meant the simple commodity economy of small producers. Under capitalism, however, the value of a commodity is from income: wages, profits, and rents. Such a statement reflected the deceptive appearance of the phenomena of the capitalist economy. Smith believed that the value of the entire social product consists only of income - wages, profits, and rent, that is, he erroneously omitted the value of the constant capital consumed in the production of goods. This "Smith's dogma" ruled out any possibility of understanding the process of social reproduction.

Smith first outlined the class structure of capitalist society, pointing out that it falls into three classes: 1) workers, 2) capitalists, and 3) landowners. But Smith was limited by the bourgeois outlook and reflected in his views the underdevelopment of the class struggle of that era; he argued that a community of interests dominates in capitalist society, since everyone strives for their own benefit, and a common benefit arises from the collision of individual aspirations.

Strongly opposed to the theoretical views and policies of the mercantilists, Smith ardently defended free competition.

In the writings of David Ricardo (1772-1823), bourgeois classical political economy was completed. Ricardo lived during the Industrial Revolution in England. His main work, The Principles of Political Economy and Taxation, was published in 1817.

Ricardo developed the labor theory of value with the greatest consistency possible within the bourgeois horizon. Rejecting Smith's position that value is determined by labor only in the "primitive state of society", he showed that the value created by the labor of the worker is the source   from which both wages and profit and rent arise.

Proceeding from the fact that value is determined by labor, Ricardo showed the opposition of the class interests of bourgeois society, as it manifests itself in the sphere of distribution. Ricardo considered the existence of classes an eternal phenomenon in the life of society. According to Marx, Ricardo "consciously takes as the starting point of his research the opposition of class interests, wages and profits, profits and ground rent, naively considering this opposition as a natural law of social life" [1]. Ricardo formulated an important economic law: the higher the wages of the worker, the lower the profit of the capitalist, and vice versa. Ricardo also showed the opposite of profit and rent; but he was mistaken in recognizing the existence of only differential rent, which he associated with the imaginary "law of diminishing soil fertility."

Ricardo played a large role in the development of political economy. His teaching that value is determined only by labor was of outstanding historical significance. Observing the growth of capitalist contradictions, some of his followers began to conclude: if value is created only by labor, then it is necessary and fair that the worker, the creator of all wealth, should also be the owner of all wealth, all products of labor. Such a demand was put forward in England in the first half of the 19th century by the early socialists, the followers of Ricardo.

At the same time, the teachings of Ricardo bore the features of bourgeois narrow-mindedness. The capitalist system, with its antithesis of class interests, seemed to Ricardo, as to Smith, a natural and eternal system. Ricardo did not even raise the question of the historical origin of such economic categories as goods, money, capital, profit, etc. He understood capital ahistorical way, identifying it with the means of production.

The emergence of vulgar political economy.

With the development of capitalism and the intensification of the class struggle, classical bourgeois political economy gives way to vulgar political economy. Marx called it vulgar because its representatives replaced the scientific knowledge of economic phenomena with a description of their outward appearance, aiming to embellish capitalism and gloss over its contradictions. The vulgar economists rejected everything that was scientific and took up everything that was unscientific in the views of previous economists (especially A. Smith), everything that was due to the class limitations of their horizons.

"From now on, it was no longer a matter of whether this or that theorem was right or wrong, but of whether it was useful for capital or harmful, convenient, or inconvenient, consistent with police considerations or not. Disinterested research gives way to the battles of hired hacks, impartial scientific research is replaced by biased, obsequious apologetics .

In the field of the theory of value, vulgar economics, in opposition to the determination of value by labor time, put forward a number of propositions that were already refuted by the bourgeois classical school. These include: the theory of supply and demand, which ignores the value underlying prices and replaces the explanation of the very basis of the prices of goods with a description of the fluctuations of these prices; the theory of production costs, which explains the prices of some goods with the help of the prices of other goods, that is, in fact, rotates in a vicious circle; a theory of utility which, in attempting to explain the value of commodities by their use-value, ignores the fact that the use-values of heterogeneous commodities are qualitatively different and therefore quantitatively incomparable.

The English vulgar economist T. - R. Malthus (1766 - 1834) came up with the fabrication that the poverty of the broad masses of working people, characteristic of capitalism, is due to the fact that people multiply faster than the amount of means of subsistence delivered by nature can increase. According to Malthus, the necessary correspondence between the size of the population and the amount of livelihood delivered by nature is established by hunger, poverty, epidemics, and wars. The misanthropic "theory" of Malthus was created to justify a social order in which the parasitism and luxury of the exploiting

102

classes coexist with backbreaking labor and the growing need of the broad masses of working people.

French vulgar economist J-B. Say (1767 - 1832) declared the source of value to be "three factors of production" - labor, capital, and land, concluding from this that the owners of each of the three factors of production receive income "owing" to them: the worker - wages, the capitalist - profit (or interest), landowner - rent. Saying that under capitalism there is no contradiction between production and consumption, Say denied the possibility of general crises of overproduction. Say's theory was a gross distortion of reality to please the exploiting classes. The fabrications about the harmony of class interests under capitalism were diligently disseminated by the French economist F. Bastiat (1801 - 1850) and the American C. Carey (1793 - 1879). Under the pretext of defending bourgeois "freedom of labour," vulgar political economy waged a fierce struggle against trade unions, collective agreements, and workers' strikes. From the second quarter of the 19th century, vulgar political economy gained undivided dominance in bourgeois science.

Petty-bourgeois political economy.

At the beginning of the 19th century, a petty-bourgeois trend in political economy emerged, reflecting the contradictory position of the petty bourgeoisie as an intermediate class in capitalist society. Petty-bourgeois political economy originates from the Swiss economist S. Sismondi (1773 - 1842). Unlike Smith and Ricardo, who considered the capitalist system to be the natural state of society, Sismondi criticized capitalism, condemning it from the positions of the petty bourgeoisie.

Sismondi idealized the petty commodity production of peasants and artisans and came up with utopian projects to perpetuate small property, not seeing the inevitability of the growth of capitalist relations inherent in petty commodity production. From the fact that the incomes of workers and small producers are declining, Sismondi erroneously concluded that the market would inevitably shrink as capitalism developed. He incorrectly argued that the accumulation of capital is possible only in the presence of small producers and an external market.

The views of petty-bourgeois political economy were developed in France by P.-J-Proudhon (1809-1865). He defended the reactionary idea of curing all the social evils of capitalism by setting up a special bank that would carry out a non-monetary exchange of the products of small producers and would provide free credit to the workers. Proudhon sowed reformist illusions among the working masses, diverting them from the class struggle.

In Russia at the end of the 19th century, the reactionary-utopian ideas of petty-bourgeois political economy were preached by liberal populists.

Utopian socialists.

With the advent and development of large-scale machine industry at the end of the 18th and beginning of the 19th century, the contradictions of capitalism and the disasters that it brings to the working masses became more and more clearly revealed. But the working class was not yet aware of its historical role as the grave-digger of capitalism. During this period, the great utopian socialists acted: Henri Saint-Simon (1760 - 1825) and Charles Fourier (1772 - 1837) in France, Robert Owen (1771 - 1858) in England, who played a major role in the history of the development of socialist ideas.

In explaining economic phenomena, the utopian socialists remained on the same soil of the eighteenth-century enlightenment philosophy on which the representatives of bourgeois classical political economy stood. But while the latter considered the capitalist system to be in accordance with human nature, the utopian socialists viewed this system as contrary to human nature.

The historical significance of the utopian socialists lay in the fact that they subjected bourgeois society to resolute criticism, mercilessly scourging its ulcers such as poverty and deprivation of the masses, doomed to hard, exhausting work, venality, and decay of the rich elite of society, a huge waste of productive forces as a result of competition, crises, etc. To the capitalist system based on private ownership of the means of production and the exploitation of some classes of society by others, the utopian socialists opposed the coming socialist system based on public ownership of the means of production and free from the exploitation of man by man. But the utopian socialists were far from understanding the real ways of realizing socialism.

Not knowing the laws of social development, the laws of the class struggle, they believed that the propertied classes themselves would realize socialism when they could be convinced of the rationality, justice, and expediency of this new system. The understanding of the historical role of the proletariat was completely alien to the utopian socialists. Utopian socialism "could neither explain the essence of wage slavery under capitalism, nor discover the laws of its development, nor find that a social force capable of becoming the creator of a new society" [3] .

Revolutionary democrats in Russia.

In the middle of the 19th century in Russia, which was experiencing a crisis of serfdom, a brilliant galaxy of thinkers emerged who made a great contribution to the development of economic science.

AI Herzen (1812 - 1870) castigated tsarism and serfdom in Russia, calling on the people for a revolutionary struggle against them. He sharply criticized the system of capitalist exploitation that had taken root in the West. Herzen laid the foundation for utopian "peasant socialism". He saw "socialism" in the liberation of the peasants with land, in communal land ownership and in the peasant idea of "the right to land." There was nothing really socialist in these views of Herzen, but they expressed the revolutionary aspirations of the Russian peasantry, who fought to overthrow the power of the landowners and to abolish landownership.

The great Russian revolutionary and scientist N.G. Chernyshevsky (1828-1889) has made enormous contributions to the development of economics. Chernyshevsky led the decisive struggle of the revolutionary democrats against serfdom and the tsarist autocracy in Russia. He gave a brilliant critique not only of serfdom, but also of the capitalist system, which by that time had become established in Western Europe and North America. Chernyshevsky deeply revealed the class character and limitations of bourgeois classical political economy and subjected to devastating criticism the vulgar economists - John Stuart Mill, Say, Malthus and others. According to Marx, N. G. Chernyshevsky skillfully explained the bankruptcy of bourgeois political economy.

Bourgeois political economy, which serves the selfish interests of the capitalists, Chernyshevsky opposed the "political economy of the working people", in which labor and the interests of the working people should take a central place. Being a representative of utopian "peasant socialism", Chernyshevsky, in view of the underdevelopment of capitalist relations in contemporary Russia, did not see that the development of capitalism and the proletariat creates material conditions and social strength for the implementation of socialism. But Chernyshevsky, in understanding the nature of capitalist society and its class structure, the nature of its economic development, went far ahead in comparison with the Western European utopian socialists and took a major step towards scientific socialism. Unlike the utopian socialists of the West, Chernyshevsky attached decisive importance to the revolutionary activity of the working masses, their struggle for their liberation, and called for a people's revolution against the exploiters. Chernyshevsky was a consistent, militant revolutionary democrat. Lenin wrote that his writings emanate the spirit of the class struggle.

The economic doctrine of Chernyshevsky represents the pinnacle of the development of all political economy before Marx. In his philosophical views Chernyshevsky was a militant materialist. Like Herzen, he came close to dialectical materialism.

The revolutionary democrats - Herzen, Chernyshevsky and their like-minded people were the forerunners of the Russian Social Democracy.

Revolutionary upheaval in political economy accomplished by K. Marx and F. Engels.

By the middle of the 19th century, the capitalist economic system had become dominant in the principal countries of Western Europe and in the United States of America. A proletariat took shape and began to rise up to fight against the bourgeoisie. Conditions arose for the creation of an advanced proletarian worldview - scientific socialism.

Karl Marx (1818-1883) and Friedrich Engels (1820-1895) turned socialism from a utopia into a science. The doctrine worked out by Marx and Engels expresses the fundamental interests of the working class and is the banner of the struggle of the proletarian masses for the revolutionary overthrow of capitalism, for the victory of socialism. Marx's teaching "arose as a direct and immediate continuation of the teachings of the greatest representatives of philosophy, political economy and socialism"[4].

The genius of Marx, as Lenin pointed out, lies precisely in the fact that he gave answers to questions that the progressive thought of mankind had already posed. His teaching is the legitimate successor to the best that has been created by human thought in the field of the science of human society. At the same time, the emergence of Marxism was a radical revolutionary change in philosophy, in political economy, in all social sciences. Marx and Engels armed the working class with a coherent and harmonious worldview - dialectical materialism, which is the theoretical foundation of scientific communism.

By extending dialectical materialism to the realm of social phenomena, they created historical materialism, which is the greatest achievement of scientific thought. They opposed the non-historical approach to human society with a historical approach based on a deep study of the actual course of development. They replaced the previously dominant idea of the immutability, immobility of society with a coherent doctrine that reveals the objective laws of social development - the laws of the replacement of one form of society by another. Marx and Engels were the founders of a truly scientific political economy. By applying the method of dialectical materialism to the study of economic relations, Marx brought about the most profound revolutionary change in political economy.

Approaching political economy as the ideologist of the working class, Marx revealed to the end the contradictions of capitalism and created proletarian political economy. Marx created his economic doctrine in an uncompromising struggle against the bourgeois apology for capitalism and petty-bourgeois criticism of it. Using and developing a number of provisions of the classics of bourgeois political economy - Smith and Ricardo, Marx decisively overcame the anti-scientific views and contradictions contained in their teaching. In his economic teaching, Marx summed up and generalized the gigantic material on the history of human society and, in particular, on the history of the emergence and development of capitalism.

Marx is credited with the discovery of the historically transient nature of the capitalist mode of production and the study of the laws of the rise, development, and death of capitalism. Based on a deep economic analysis of the capitalist system, Marx substantiated the historical mission of the proletariat as the gravedigger of capitalism and the creator of a new, socialist society.

The foundations of the Marxist worldview were already proclaimed in the first program document of scientific communism - in the "Manifesto of the Communist Party", written by Marx and Engels in 1848. Marx published the results of his further economic research in the work "On the Critique of Political Economy" (1859), dedicated to analysis of goods and money; the preface to this work gives a classic exposition of the foundations of historical materialism. Marx's main work, which he rightfully called his life's work, is Capital. The first volume of Capital (The Process of Production of Capital) was published by Marx in 1867; the second volume (The Process of Circulation of Capital) was published by Engels after the death of Marx, in 1885, and the third volume (The Process of Capitalist Production Taken as a Whole) in 1894. While working on Capital, Marx intended to write a fourth volume devoted to a critical analysis of the history of political economy. The preparatory manuscripts he left were published after the death of Marx and Engels under the title "Theories of surplus value" (in three volumes).

A number of Engels' classical works are also devoted to the development of the theory of scientific communism. These include: "The Condition of the Working Class in England" (1845), "Anti-Dühring" (1878), which dealt with the most important issues from the field of philosophy, natural science, and social sciences, "The Origin of the Family, Private Property and the State" (1884) and others.

In creating proletarian political economy, Marx first of all substantiated and consistently developed the labor theory of value. Investigating the commodity, the contradiction between its use value and value, Marx discovered that the labor contained in the commodity has a dual character. It is, on the one hand, concrete labor that creates the use value of a commodity, and, on the other hand, abstract labor that creates its value. The revelation of the dual character of labor served Marx as the key to the scientific explanation of all the phenomena of the capitalist mode of production on the basis of the labor theory of value. Having shown that value is not a thing, but the production relation of people, covered with a material shell, Marx revealed the secret of commodity fetishism. He analyzed the form of value, studied its historical development from the first rudiments of exchange to the complete dominance of commodity production, which enabled him to reveal the real nature of money.

The labor theory of value served as the basis for Marx's theory of surplus value. Marx was the first to show that under capitalism the commodity is not labor, but labor power. He investigated the value and use value of this specific commodity and explained the nature of capitalist exploitation. Marx's theory of surplus value completely reveals the essence of the main production relation of capitalism - the relationship between the capitalist and the worker, reveals the deepest foundations of class opposition and the class struggle between the proletariat and the bourgeoisie.

Marx not only revealed the origin and source of surplus value, but also explained how capitalist exploitation is masked and obscured. He investigated the essence of wages as the price of labor power, acting in a transformed form of the price of labor.

Marx gave a deep scientific analysis of the various forms that surplus value takes. He showed how surplus value appears in a transformed form, in the form of profit, and how it further takes the form of land rent and interest. Moreover, a deceptive appearance is created, as if wages are the price of labor, as if profit is generated by capital itself, rent by land and interest by money.

In his doctrine of the price of production and average profit, Marx resolved the contradiction that, under capitalism, market prices deviate from value. At the same time, he revealed the objective basis of the solidarity of the capitalist class with regard to the exploitation of workers, since the average profit received by each capitalist is determined by the degree of exploitation not in a single enterprise, but in the entire capitalist society.

Marx developed the theory of differential rent and for the first time gave a scientific justification for the theory of absolute rent. He explained the reactionary, parasitic role of large land ownership, the essence, and forms of exploitation of the peasants by the landowners and the bourgeoisie.

Marx first revealed the laws of capitalist accumulation, establishing that the development of capitalism, the concentration and centralization of capital inevitably leads to a deepening and aggravation of the contradictions inherent in this system, which are based on the contradiction between the social nature of production and the private capitalist form of appropriation. Marx discovered the universal law of capitalist accumulation, which determines the growth of wealth and luxury at one pole of society and the growth of poverty, oppression, and labor pain at the other pole. He showed that with the development of capitalism, there is a relative and absolute impoverishment of the proletariat, which leads to a deepening of the gulf between the proletariat and the bourgeoisie, to an intensification of the class struggle between them.

Marx's analysis of the reproduction of all social capital is of the utmost importance . Having eliminated Smith's mistake, which consisted in ignoring the constant capital consumed in the production of goods, establishing the division of the social product according to value into three parts $(c + v + m)$, and according to the natural form - into the means of production and consumer goods, Marx analyzed the conditions of simple and expanded capitalist reproduction, deep contradictions of capitalist realization, inevitably leading to crises of overproduction. He investigated the nature of economic crises and scientifically proved their inevitability under capitalism.

The economic doctrine of Marx and Engels is a deep and comprehensive justification for the inevitability of the collapse of capitalism and the victory of the proletarian revolution, which establishes the dictatorship of the working class and opens a new era - the era of building a socialist society.

Already in the 70s and 80s of the XIX century, Marxism began to receive more and more recognition among the working class and the advanced intelligentsia of the capitalist countries. Paul Lafargue (1842 - 1911) in France, Wilhelm Liebknecht (1826 - 1900) and August Bebel (1840 - 1913) in Germany, G. V. Plekhanov (1856 - 1918) in Russia played an important role in spreading the ideas of Marxism in those years. , Dmitry Blagoev (1855 - 1924) in Bulgaria and other prominent figures of the labor movement in various countries.

In Russia, the Marxist Workers' Party and its world outlook took shape in an uncompromising struggle against the bitterest enemy of Marxism; populism.

The Narodniks denied the leading role of the proletariat in the revolutionary movement: they asserted that the development of capitalism was allegedly impossible in Russia. Plekhanov and the Emancipation of Labor group, organized by him, spoke out against the Narodniks. Plekhanov was the first to give a Marxist critique of the erroneous views of the Narodniks and at the same time launched a brilliant defense of Marxist views. Plekhanov's activities in the 1880s and 1890s were of great importance for the ideological training of proletarian revolutionaries in Russia. In a number of works, Plekhanov successfully popularized certain aspects of Marx's economic doctrine, defending this doctrine from bourgeois criticism and reformist perversions. Plekhanov's literary works thoroughly undermined the position of the Narodniks.

But the ideological defeat of populism was not completed. Already in the early period of his activity, Plekhanov had an erroneous understanding of a number of issues, which was the embryo of his future Menshevik views: he did not take into account that in the course of the revolution the proletariat should lead the peasantry, he considered the liberal bourgeoisie as a force that could support the revolution, etc. The task of finishing off populism as the enemy of Marxism and uniting Marxism with the workers' movement in Russia was solved by Lenin.

Further decomposition of bourgeois economic science. Modern bourgeois political economy.

From the time that Marxism entered the historical arena, the main and decisive task of bourgeois economists has been the "refutation" of Marxism.

In Germany in the middle of the 19th century, the so-called historical school of political economy arose (W. Roscher, B. Hildebrand , and others). Representatives of this school openly denied the existence of economic laws of the development of society and replaced scientific research with a description of disparate historical facts. The denial of economic laws served these economists as a justification for any reactionary arbitrariness, groveling before the military-bureaucratic state, which they exalted in every possible way.

Later representatives of the historical school, headed by G. Schmoller , formed the so-called historical-ethical or historical-legal direction. A characteristic feature of this trend, also called katheder-socialism (literally "socialism of the pulpit"), is the substitution of economic research for reactionary-idealist chatter about moral goals, legal norms, etc. Continuing the traditions of their predecessors, katheder-socialists acted as servants of the militaristic German state , each event of which they declared "a piece of socialism." The Katheder Socialists glorified Bismarck's reactionary policies and helped him to deceive the working class.

In the last decades of the 19th century, as the ideas of Marxism spread, the bourgeoisie needed new ideological means to fight them. Then the so-called Austrian school appeared on the scene. The name of this school is due to the fact that its main representatives - K. Menger, F. Wieser and E. Böhm-Bawerk - were professors at Austrian universities. In contrast to the historical direction, the representatives of the Austrian school formally recognized the need to study economic laws, but in order to embellish and protect the capitalist order, they transferred the search for these laws from the sphere of social relations to the subjective psychological area, that is, they took the path of idealism.

In the field of value theory, the Austrian school put forward the so-called "marginal utility" principle. According to this principle, the value of a commodity is determined not simply by its utility, as some vulgar economists used to say, but by the marginal utility of the commodity, that is, the least urgent of the needs of the individual, which this unit of commodity satisfies. In fact, this theory does not explain anything. It is quite obvious, for example, that the subjective evaluation of a kilogram of bread is fundamentally different for a satiated bourgeois and a hungry unemployed man, and yet both of them pay the same price for bread. To Marx's theory of surplus value, economists of the Austrian school opposed the anti-scientific "theory of imputation", which was only an updated form of the vulgar theory of the "three factors of production".

The transition to imperialism and the extreme aggravation of social contradictions and the class struggle connected with it caused a further degradation of bourgeois political economy. After the victory of the socialist revolution in the USSR, which practically refuted the assertions of the ideologists of the bourgeoisie about the eternity of the capitalist system, bourgeois economists began to see one of their main tasks in hiding from the working people of the capitalist countries the truth about the world-historical achievements of the country of socialism by slandering the Soviet Union. Modern bourgeois political economy is the ideological weapon of the financial oligarchy, it is the servant of imperialist reaction and aggression.

In explaining such categories of capitalism as value, price, wages, profit, rent, modern bourgeois economists usually take the position of the subjective-psychological direction, one of the varieties of which is the Austrian school discussed above, and rehash the old vulgar theory of three factors in different ways. production. The English economist Alfred Marshall (1842-1924) tried to eclectically reconcile three different vulgar theories of value: supply and demand, marginal utility, and cost of production. American economist John Bates Clark (1847 - 1938), preaching the false idea of "harmony of interests" of various classes of bourgeois society, put forward the theory of "marginal productivity", which in fact is only a kind of attempt to combine the old vulgar theory of "productivity of capital" with the vulgar theory of "marginal utility" of the Austrian school. Profit, according to Clarke, is supposedly a reward for the work of the entrepreneur, and the working classes create only a small share of wealth and receive it in full.

Unlike the bourgeois economists of the era of pre-monopoly capitalism, who sang of freedom of competition as the main condition for the development of society, modern bourgeois economists usually emphasize the need for all-round state intervention in economic life. They exalt the imperialist state as a force supposedly standing above classes and capable of subordinating the economy of the capitalist countries to planning. Meanwhile, in reality, the intervention of the bourgeois state in economic life has nothing in common with the planning of the national economy, and further strengthens the anarchy of production. Apologists for monopolies hypocritically pass off as "organized capitalism" the subordination of the imperialist state to the financial oligarchy,

In the first decades of the 20th century, the so-called social direction, or the socio-organic school of political economy , became widespread in Germany (A. Ammon, R. Stoltzmann, O. Spann and others). In contrast to the Austrian school with its subjective-psychological approach to economic phenomena, representatives of the social direction talked about the social relations of people, but they considered these relations idealistically, as legal forms devoid of any material content. Economists of the social direction argued that social life was supposedly governed by legal and ethical norms. They covered up their zealous service to the capitalist monopolies with demagogic arguments about the "common good" and the need to subjugate the "part", that is, the working masses, to the "whole", that is, the imperialist state. They extolled the activity of the capitalists, declaring it a service to society. The reactionary fabrications of this school served as an ideological weapon for fascism in Germany and other bourgeois countries.

German fascism used the most reactionary elements of German vulgar political economy, its extreme chauvinism, admiration for the bourgeois state, preaching the conquest of foreign lands and "class peace" within Germany. Being the worst enemies of socialism and all progressive mankind, the German fascists resorted to anti-capitalist demagogy and hypocritically called themselves National Socialists. Italian and German fascists preached the reactionary theory of the "corporate state", according to which capitalism, classes and class contradictions were supposedly eliminated in fascist countries. Nazi economists justified the predatory practice of seizing foreign lands by Nazi Germany with the help of the so-called "racial theory" and the "theory of living space." According to these "theories", the Germans are allegedly the "superior race", and all other nations are "inferior", and the "race of masters" supposedly has the right to seize the lands of other, "inferior" peoples by force and extend their dominance to the whole world. Historical experience has clearly shown all the absurdity and impracticability of Hitler's crazy plans for the conquest of world domination.

During the period of the general crisis of capitalism, when the problem of the market became unprecedentedly acute, economic crises became more frequent and deepened, permanent mass unemployment arose, various theories appeared that inspired the illusion that it was possible to ensure "full employment", eliminate the anarchy of production and crises while maintaining the capitalist system. The theory of the English economist J. M. Keynes (1883-1946), which he outlined in his book The General Theory of Employment, Interest and Money (1936), was widely adopted among bourgeois economists .

Obscuring the real causes of constant mass unemployment and crises under capitalism, Keynes seeks to prove that the cause of these "flaws" of bourgeois society lies not in the nature of capitalism, but in the psychology of people. According to Keynes, unemployment is the result of insufficient demand for personal and industrial consumption. The lack of consumer demand is caused, as it were, by the propensity inherent in people to save a part of their income, and the lack of demand for articles of industrial consumption is caused by the weakening of the capitalists' interest in applying their capital in various branches of the economy due to the general decrease in the "profitability of capital". In order to increase employment, Keynes argues, it is necessary to expand investment, for which the state must, on the one hand, ensure the growth of the profitability of capital by lowering the real wages of workers, by means of inflation and lowering the rate of loan interest, and, on the other hand, by making large capital investments at the expense of the budget. To expand consumer demand, Keynes recommends a further increase in the parasitic consumption and squandering of the ruling classes, an increase in spending on military purposes and on other unproductive expenditures of the state.

Keynes's theory is completely untenable and profoundly reactionary in its essence. The lack of consumer demand is caused not by the mythical "inclination of people to save", but by the impoverishment of the working people. The measures proposed by Keynes supposedly in the interests of ensuring full employment of the population - inflation, the growth of unproductive costs for preparing and conducting wars - actually lead to a further decrease in the living standards of the working people, to a narrowing of the market and an increase in unemployment. The vulgar theory of Keynes is now widely used by bourgeois economists, as well as by right-wing socialists in the USA, Britain, and other capitalist countries.

The modern vulgar political economy of the United States is characterized by a theory that promotes the growth of the state budget and public debt as a means of overcoming the vices of capitalism. American economist A. Hansen, Considering that the possibilities for the further development of capitalism through the action of spontaneous economic forces alone are significantly narrowed, he proves the need for "regulation" of the capitalist economy by the state by forcing capital investments through increased state orders. He preaches organization at the expense of the state budget, that is, at the expense of taxes and loans, public works, which supposedly should provide "general employment" and improve modern capitalism. In fact, in the context of the preparations by the imperialist powers for a new world war, this kind of "public work" means nothing more than the construction of strategic highways, railways, airfields, naval bases, etc., that is, the further militarization of the economy and, associated with thereby exacerbating the contradictions of imperialism.

Some bourgeois economists in the USA and Britain advocate "the free play of economic forces," by which they actually mean the unlimited freedom of the monopolies to exploit the workers and rob consumers. These economists hypocritically declare the activity of the trade unions in defense of the workers a violation of "economic freedom" and praise the reactionary anti-worker legislation of the imperialist states. Both the heralds of the "regulation" of the economy by the bourgeois state and the

121

defenders of the "free play of economic forces" express the interests of the financial oligarchy, which seeks to secure maximum profit for itself by further intensifying the exploitation of the working masses at home and by imperialist aggression in the international arena.

Bourgeois economists try to justify the predatory policy of the imperialist powers seizing foreign lands, enslaving, and robbing other peoples with anti-scientific fabrications about the "unequal value" of different races and nations, about the civilizing mission of the "higher" races and nations in relation to the "lower", etc. They are especially zealous in this respect, reactionary American economists who, following in the footsteps of the German fascists, spread the misanthropic idea of the "superiority" of English-speaking nations over all other peoples and strive in every possible way to justify the crazy plans for establishing US world domination.

The reverse side of the racial theory is bourgeois cosmopolitanism, which denies the principle of the equality of nations and demands the destruction of state borders. Bourgeois cosmopolitans declare national sovereignty, the independence of peoples an obsolete concept, and proclaim the existence of nation-states as the main cause of all social disasters of modern bourgeois society - militarism, wars, unemployment, poverty of people, etc. They oppose the cosmopolitan idea of a "world state" to the principle of national sovereignty of peoples , in which they invariably assign the United States the leading role. The same goal of eliminating the national sovereignty of the European peoples and completely subordinating them to the domination of the US imperialists is pursued by the intensified propaganda of the idea of a "united Europe", a "United States of Europe".

Many US bourgeois economists come out with direct propaganda of a new world war. They declare war to be a natural and eternal phenomenon of social life, asserting that the peaceful coexistence of the countries of the capitalist camp and the countries of the socialist camp is impossible.

In order to justify imperialist aggression and to prepare for a new world war, the long-unmasked theory of Malthus is widely propagated in bourgeois literature. Modern Malthusianism is characterized by a combination of the reactionary ideas of Malthus with racial theory. The Malthusians of the United States and other bourgeois countries assert that the globe is overpopulated as a result of the "excessive reproduction" of people, which is the root cause of hunger and all other calamities of the working masses. They demand a sharp reduction in population, especially in colonial and dependent countries whose peoples are waging a liberation struggle against imperialism. Modern Malthusians call for devastating wars with the use of atomic bombs and other means of mass extermination of people.

All these statements of the apologists of capitalism serve as clear evidence of the complete bankruptcy of modern bourgeois political economy.

Economic theories of the opportunists of the Second International and contemporary right-wing socialists.

The countless attempts of bourgeois science to "destroy" Marxism did not in the least shake its positions. Then the struggle against Marxism began to be waged in a double-dealing way, clothed in the form of "improvements" and "interpretations" of Marx's theory. "The dialectic of history is such that the theoretical victory of Marxism forces its enemies to disguise themselves as Marxists" [5] .

In the 90s of the 19th century, revisionism appeared on the scene, the main representative of which was the German Social Democrat E. Bernstein. The revisionists took up arms against the teachings of Marx and Engels on the inevitability of the revolutionary downfall of capitalism and the establishment of the dictatorship of the proletariat. They subjected to a complete revision (revision) all parts of the revolutionary economic teachings of Marx. The revisionists proposed to combine Marx's labor theory of value with the theory of marginal utility, and, in essence, to replace it with the latter.

They interpreted the Marxist doctrine of surplus value in the sense of "moral condemnation" of capitalist exploitation. Under the guise of supposedly "new data" on the development of capitalism, the revisionists declared "outdated" Marx's doctrine of the victory of large-scale production over small production, of the impoverishment of the proletariat in capitalist society, of irreconcilability and aggravation of class contradictions, and of the inevitability of economic crises of overproduction under capitalism.

They called on the workers to abandon the revolutionary struggle for the destruction of the capitalist system and confine themselves to the struggle for current economic interests. In Russia, the views of revisionism were taken up by the so-called "legal Marxists", who were in fact bourgeois ideologists.(P. Struve, M. Tugan-Baranovsky and others), representatives of the opportunist group of "economists" and the Mensheviks.

A more subtle form of distortion of Marxism was used by the opportunists of the Second International K. Kautsky (1854-1938), R. Hilferding (1877 - 1941) and others. At the beginning of their activities, they were Marxists, contributing to the spread of Marxist teachings. In the future, they actually switched to the position of opponents of revolutionary Marxism, continuing for the time being to act under the guise of "orthodox", that is, allegedly orthodox disciples of Marx and Engels. By objecting verbally - and then very inconsistently - against certain assertions of the revisionists, these opportunists emasculated the revolutionary essence of Marxism and tried to turn Marxism into a dead dogma. They rejected the doctrine of the dictatorship of the proletariat, which is the soul of Marxism, they denied the absolute impoverishment of the working class, they asserted that crises under capitalism become rarer and weaker. The revisionists sought to adapt proletarian political economy to the interests of the bourgeoisie.

In order to gloss over the deep contradictions of monopoly capitalism, K. Kautsky interpreted imperialism only as a special kind of politics, namely, as the desire of highly developed industrial countries to subjugate the agrarian regions. This theory sowed illusions about the possibility of a different, non-aggressive policy under monopoly capitalism. During the First

World War, Kautsky came up with the anti-Marxist theory of ultra-imperialism (super-imperialism), arguing that under imperialism it is possible, through collusion between the capitalists of different countries, to eliminate wars and create an organized world economy. This reactionary theory is characterized by the separation of economics from politics and ignorance of the law of uneven development of the capitalist countries in the era of imperialism. The theory of "ultra-imperialism" embellished imperialism and disarmed the working class to please the bourgeoisie, creating illusions about the possibility of a peaceful and crisis-free development of capitalism.

The same goal was served by the vulgar "theory of productive forces" preached by Kautsky, according to which socialism is supposedly a mechanical result of the development of the productive forces of society, without class struggle and revolution.

R. Hilferding in his work Finance Capital (1910), devoted to the study of the "recent phase of capitalism", giving a scientific analysis of some aspects of the economy of imperialism, at the same time obscured the decisive role of monopolies in modern capitalism and the aggravation of all its contradictions, ignored the most important the features of imperialism are parasitism and the decay of capitalism, the division of the world and the struggle for its redistribution. During the years of temporary, partial stabilization of capitalism, Hilferding, following the bourgeois economists, argued that the era of "organized capitalism" had begun, when competition, anarchy of production, and crises disappear due to the activity of monopolies, and planned, conscious organization begins to dominate. Hence the reactionary leaders of the Social Democracy concluded that trusts and cartels were peacefully "growing" into a planned socialist economy;

Thus, the embellishment of imperialism by Kautsky, Hilferding and other reformist theorists of Social Democracy is inextricably linked with their preaching of the "peaceful growth of capitalism into socialism", aimed at diverting the working class from the tasks of the revolutionary struggle for socialism, towards subordinating the labor movement to the interests of the imperialist bourgeoisie. This goal was served, in particular, by the apologetic theory of "economic democracy" spread by some right-wing socialist leaders between the two world wars. According to this theory, workers, acting as representatives of trade unions in factory management and other bodies, allegedly take an equal part in the management of the economy and gradually become the masters of production.

A variation of the reformist theory of the peaceful growth of capitalism into socialism is the theory of "cooperative socialism", built on the illusion that, while maintaining the dominance of capital, the spread of cooperative forms would allegedly lead to socialism.

In Russia, anti-Marxist, Kautskyian views on questions of the theory of imperialism were spread by the enemies of socialism—the Mensheviks, Trotskyists, Bukharinites, and others. Preaching apologetic theories of "pure imperialism", "organized capitalism", etc., they sought to cover up the growing contradictions of monopoly capitalism. Denying the law of the uneven development of capitalism in the era of imperialism, they tried to poison the consciousness of the working class with the poison of disbelief in the possibility of the victory of socialism in one country.

In the period after the Second World War, right-wing reformist leaders of the British Labor Party, right-wing socialist leaders in France, Italy, West Germany, Austria, and other countries (L. Blum, K. Renner) acted as defenders of capitalism . and others). Acting as agents of the imperialist bourgeoisie in the workers' movement, the leaders of the right-wing socialists defend the monopolies, preach a class peace between the workers and the bourgeoisie, and actively support the reactionary domestic and aggressive foreign policy of imperialism. In an effort to reconcile the working people with imperialism, to inspire the working class with faith in the possibility of improving its plight while maintaining the capitalist system, right-wing socialist theorists have composed the theory of "democratic socialism", which is a version of the theory of the peaceful growth of capitalism into socialism.

The theory of "democratic socialism" asserts that in England, in the USA, in France and in other capitalist countries there is no longer any exploitation and opposition between the class interests of the proletariat and the bourgeoisie, moreover, the imperialist state is declared a supra-class organization, and any enterprise that is the property of this state, - "socialist" enterprise. The Labor leaders proclaimed the nationalization of the Bank of England, the railways, and certain branches of industry, carried out during their time in power after the Second World War, as a triumph of "democratic socialism". In reality, the Labor nationalization was a bourgeois measure that did not change the economic nature of the nationalized enterprises as capitalist enterprises. The real masters in

England continued to be the imperialist bourgeoisie and the big landowners, the landlords. Owners of previously unprofitable nationalized enterprises have received generous compensation and high income security, and workers in the nationalized industries are forced to work even harder at low wages. The theory of "democratic socialism" serves as a screen covering the growing oppression of the working masses by state-monopoly capitalism, which is the highest stage of domination by the financial oligarchy.

While preaching "class peace" in capitalist society, the leaders of the right-wing socialist parties are at the same time actively helping the bourgeoisie to carry out a broad offensive against the living standards of the working masses, to stifle the labor movement in the metropolitan countries and the national liberation movement in the colonies and dependent countries. In interpreting and evaluating all the most important economic phenomena of the modern era, they follow in the footsteps of the bourgeois economists.

A consistent struggle against the reactionary "theories" of bourgeois economists and right-wing socialist leaders is waged by communist workers' parties, which are guided in their activities by the theory of Marxism-Leninism.

The ideas of progressive Marxist-Leninist theory are becoming more and more widespread among the progressive part of the intelligentsia of the capitalist countries, including among economists. An army of advanced scientists and public figures of various views and directions is growing and multiplying, taking an active part in the struggle for the national independence of their peoples, for peace, for the development of economic and cultural ties between all countries, regardless of differences in their social system.

The development of the Marxist political economy of capitalism by VI Lenin. Development of a number of new provisions of the political economy of capitalism by IV Stalin.

The economic doctrine of Marx and Engels received its further creative development in the works of V. I. Lenin (1870 - 1924). Marx, Engels, Lenin are the creators of truly scientific political economy. As a faithful follower and continuer of the teachings of Marx and Engels, Lenin launched an uncompromising struggle against the open and hidden enemies of Marxism. Lenin defended the revolutionary teachings of Marx and Engels from the attacks of bourgeois pseudoscience, from its distortions by revisionists and opportunists of all stripes. Based on the generalization of the new historical experience of the class struggle of the proletariat, he raised the teaching of Marxism to a new, higher level.

Lenin entered the arena of political struggle in the 90s of the 19th century, when the transition from pre-monopoly capitalism to imperialism was being completed, when the center of the world revolutionary movement moved to Russia, a country in which the greatest people's revolution was brewing.

In the works of the 90s - "On the so-called question of the markets" (1893), "What are the "friends of the people" and how do they fight against the social democrats?" (1894), "The economic content of populism and criticism of it in the book of Mr. Struve" (1894), "On the characteristics of economic romanticism" (1897) - Lenin consistently fought both against the populists and against the "legal Marxists" who glorified capitalism, glossed over its profound contradictions, and sought to subordinate the growing working-class movement to the interests of the bourgeoisie. The ideological defeat of populism was completed by Lenin's classic work The Development of Capitalism in Russia (1899), which is the largest work of Marxist literature since the publication of Marx's Capital.

In this work and in other works of the 1990s, Lenin gave a deep analysis of the Russian economy, revealed the economic foundations of class contradictions and class struggle, and the prospects for the revolutionary movement. Summarizing the experience of the economic and political development of Russia and other countries in the last decades of the 19th century, Lenin defended and developed the provisions of Marxism on the laws of the emergence and development of the capitalist mode of production, on its insoluble contradictions and inevitable death. Having refuted populist fabrications about the "artificiality" of Russian capitalism, Lenin revealed the peculiar features of the economy and social system of Russia, connected with the peculiarities of its historical development, in particular, the combination of methods of capitalist exploitation with numerous remnants of feudal oppression, which gave social relations in Russia a special urgency.

In the struggle against the scornful attitude of populism towards the proletariat, Lenin showed that the development of capitalism inevitably leads to an increase in the number, organization, and consciousness of the working class, which is the vanguard of the entire mass of working and exploited people. He comprehensively substantiated the leading role of the proletariat in the revolution.

Lenin found out the essence of the processes of differentiation of the peasantry in post-reform Russia and the close interweaving of the remnants of feudal bondage with the oppression of capitalist relations, refuting the populist idea of the peasantry as a homogeneous mass. He gave an economic substantiation of the possibility and necessity of a revolutionary alliance of the working class with the working and exploited masses of the peasantry.

Lenin revealed the economic basis of those features of the Russian revolution that made it a revolution of a new type - a bourgeois-democratic revolution under the hegemony of the proletariat, which had the prospect of developing into a socialist revolution.

The Development of Capitalism in Russia summarizes a number of Lenin's works on the theory of capitalist reproduction. In these works, he shattered the Simmondist assertions of the populists about the impossibility of realizing surplus value without the presence of small producers and a foreign market, and gave a comprehensive justification for the Marxist position that the market for capitalism is created in the course of the development of capitalism itself. Lenin further developed Marxist propositions on the contradictions of capitalist realization, on the growth of the organic composition of capital as a factor in the impoverishment of the proletariat, and on the inevitability of periodic crises of overproduction under capitalism.

The most valuable contribution to Marxist political economy is Lenin's work on the agrarian question, in which extensive material on the development of capitalism in agriculture in Russia and a number of other countries (France, Germany, Denmark, the USA, etc.) is scientifically summarized. In his works The Agrarian Question and the "Critiques of Marx" (1901-1907), The Agrarian Program of Social Democracy in the First Russian Revolution of 1905-1907 (1907), New Data on the Laws of the Development of Capitalism in Agriculture "(1914 - 1915) and others, Lenin deeply and comprehensively studied the laws of the capitalist development of agriculture, which were outlined by Marx only in general terms.

In the struggle against Western European and Russian revisionism, which declared agriculture to be that area of the economy where the laws of the concentration and centralization of capital were allegedly inapplicable, Lenin gave a scientific analysis of the peculiarities of the development of capitalism in the countryside. He showed the profound contradictory nature of the economic position of the main peasant masses and the inevitability of their ruin in bourgeois society. Lenin defended and developed the Marxist theory of differential and absolute land rent! Having revealed the significance of absolute rent as one of the most important factors hindering the development of productive forces in agriculture, Lenin comprehensively developed the question of the possibility, conditions, and economic consequences of land nationalization in bourgeois-democratic and socialist revolutions.

He exposed the bourgeois economists, who preached the pseudoscientific "law of diminishing fertility of the soil."

Fighting against the opportunist line of the Western European parties of the Second International and Russian Menshevism, including Trotskyism, in relation to the peasantry, Lenin substantiated the need for such a policy of the working class, which is designed to turn the bulk of the peasantry into an ally of the revolutionary proletariat.

The Leninist theory of the agrarian question was a deep economic justification for the policy of the Communist Party of Russia in the field of relations between the proletariat and the peasantry, and in particular its programmatic demand for the nationalization of the land. Lenin's works on the agrarian question form the theoretical basis of the agrarian program and agrarian policy of the fraternal communist parties.

Of great importance for the development of Marxist theory is the struggle that Lenin waged in defense of dialectical and historical materialism in his famous work Materialism and Empirio-Criticism. This book dealt a crushing blow to the very roots of the revisionist "theories" - their idealistic philosophy.

Lenin exposed the complete inconsistency of the revisionist critique of Marxist political economy. He showed the bankruptcy of revisionism in all the fundamental questions of the political economy of capitalism - in the theory of value, in the theory of surplus value, in the theory of concentration of capital, in the theory of crises, etc.

Marx and Engels, who lived in the era of pre-monopoly capitalism, naturally could not give an analysis of imperialism. The great merit of the Marxist study of the monopoly stage of capitalism belongs to Lenin.

Relying on the main propositions of Capital and generalizing the new phenomena in the economies of the capitalist countries, Lenin was the first of the Marxists to give a comprehensive analysis of imperialism as the last phase of capitalism, as the eve of the social revolution of the proletariat. This analysis is contained in his classic Imperialism, the Highest Stage of Capitalism (1916) and in other works of the period of the First World War: Socialism and War, On the Slogan of the United States of Europe, On the Caricature of Marxism and on "Imperialist Economism", "Imperialism and the Split of Socialism", "The Military Program of the Proletarian Revolution".

Leninist theory of imperialism proceeds from the fact that the deepest foundation of imperialism, its economic essence, is the domination of monopolies, that imperialism is monopoly capitalism. Lenin subjected to a comprehensive study the main economic features of imperialism and the specific forms of monopoly rule. In Lenin's teaching on imperialism, on the replacement of free competition by the rule of monopolies earning high monopoly profits, on the sources and methods of securing these high monopoly profits, the basic propositions of the basic economic law of monopoly capitalism were given. Describing imperialism as a new, higher stage of capitalism, he determined the historical place of imperialism and showed that imperialism is capitalism: monopoly, parasitic or decaying and dying.

The Leninist theory of imperialism reveals the contradictions of capitalism at the monopoly stage of its development—the contradictions between labor and capital, between metropolises and colonies, between imperialist countries. It reveals the profound causes that make imperialist wars for a new redivision of the world inevitable. The aggravation and deepening of all these contradictions reaches the extreme limits beyond which the revolution begins. Lenin substantiated the just character of the liberation struggle of the peoples against imperialist oppression and enslavement.

Lenin worked out the question of state-monopoly capitalism, of subordinating the apparatus of the bourgeois state to monopolies. He showed that state-monopoly capitalism means the highest form of capitalist socialization of production and the material preparation for socialism, on the one hand, and an all-out intensification of the exploitation of the working class and all the working masses, on the other.

Lenin discovered the law of unevenness economic and political development of the capitalist countries during the period of imperialism. Proceeding from this law, he made a great scientific discovery about the possibility of breaking the chain of world imperialism at its weakest link, the conclusion about the possibility of the victory of socialism initially in several countries or even in one country taken separately and the impossibility of the simultaneous victory of socialism in all countries.

Lenin substantiated the enormous role of the peasantry as an ally of the proletariat in the revolution. Lenin worked out the national-colonial question and outlined ways to resolve it. He proved the possibility and necessity of uniting the proletarian movement in the developed countries and the national liberation movement in the colonies into a common front of struggle against the common enemy — imperialism. Lenin's theory of imperialism was the rationale for the need for a socialist revolution, substantiation of the dictatorship of the working class in the conditions of a new historical epoch, the epoch of direct decisive battles of the proletariat for socialism. Thus, Lenin created a new, complete theory of socialist revolution.   This theory served as a guide to revolutionary action   on a gigantic scale - to the Great October Socialist Revolution in the USSR.

Lenin worked out the foundations of the doctrine of the general crisis of capitalism - the historical period of the collapse of the capitalist system and the victory of the new, higher, socialist system. As early as the years of the First World War, he came to the conclusion that the era of comparatively peaceful development of capitalism had passed, that the imperialist war, which was the greatest historical crisis, was ushering in the era of socialist revolution. The war created such an immense crisis, Lenin pointed out on the eve of the Great October Socialist Revolution, that mankind faced a choice: either perish, or hand over its fate to the most revolutionary class for the fastest transition to a higher mode of production - socialism. From the fact established by Lenin that the maturation of the socialist revolution in different parts of the world capitalist system is different in time, the following conclusion follows: that the collapse of capitalism and the victory of socialism occur through the falling away from the capitalist system of individual countries, in which the working class is victorious, coming to power in close and inseparable alliance with the main working masses of the peasantry and rallying the overwhelming majority of the people around itself. Lenin substantiated the possibility and necessity of peaceful coexistence over a long historical period of two systems - capitalist and socialist.

Lenin developed the theory of imperialism and the general crisis of capitalism in an uncompromising struggle against the bourgeois economists and opportunists of the Second International. He revealed the complete theoretical groundlessness and political harmfulness of Kautsky's anti-Marxist theory of "ultra-imperialism" and its varieties presented by Trotsky and Bukharin. In the struggle against Bukharin's anti-Marxist perversions, Lenin repeatedly emphasized that "pure imperialism", without the main base of capitalism, never existed, does not exist anywhere, and never will exist.

What characterizes imperialism is precisely the combination of monopolies with exchange, the market, and competition. Rising above the old capitalism as its superstructure and direct continuation, imperialism further sharpens all the contradictions of bourgeois society.

Lenin showed the deep connection between opportunism and imperialism and exposed the political role of the opportunists as agents of the bourgeoisie in the labor movement. Lenin laid bare the roots of the opportunist currents in the working-class movement, showing that these currents grow on the basis of the bribery and corruption of the upper strata of the working class by the bourgeoisie. Lenin dealt a crushing blow to the opportunists' apologetic interpretation of state-monopoly capitalism, which they tried to pass off as "socialism". Lenin's works directed against opportunism are of great importance for the revolutionary movement, because without exposing the ideological and political content of opportunism and its treacherous role in the workers' movement, there can be no real struggle against imperialism.

The problems of Marxist-Leninist political economy were further developed and concretized in the decisions and documents of the Communist Party of the Soviet Union, in the works of I. V. Stalin   (1879 - 1953) and other associates and students of Lenin.

Relying on the works of Marx, Engels, Lenin, who created a truly scientific political economy, Stalin put forward and developed a number of new provisions in the field of economic science based on the generalization of the new experience of historical development, the new practice of the struggle of the working class and its Communist Party. At the same time, Stalin's works give a consistent defense of Marxist political economy against the enemies of revolutionary Marxism, and popularize its main problems and provisions.

Exposing the falsity of the assertions of bourgeois economists and reformists about the mitigation of the contradictions of capitalism in the course of its historical development, Stalin substantiated the inevitability of further deepening and aggravation of these contradictions, indicating the inevitability of the death of capitalism. Stalin's writings developed a number of important propositions in the area of the agrarian question.

In the fight against revisionism, Stalin, relying on new arguments, showed the complete inconsistency of the theory of "stability" of small peasant farming. Only the abolition of the system of capitalist slavery can save the peasantry from ruin and poverty. The peasant question is the question of transforming the exploited majority of the peasantry from a reserve of the bourgeoisie into a direct reserve of the revolution, into an ally of the working class fighting for the destruction of the capitalist system. In his work "Marxism and the National Question" (1913) and in other works, Stalin gave a further development of the national question. He substantiated the importance of the economic conditions of society in the formation of nations and nation-states. The common economic life of people is one of the main features of a nation. The process of the liquidation of feudalism and the development of capitalism is at the same time the process of the formation of people into nations. Stalin revealed the significance of the national market for the process of creating national states in Western Europe, and outlined the originality of the historical course of the formation of states in the East.

The Communist Party of the Soviet Union, under the leadership of the Central Committee headed by I. V. Stalin, defended the Marxist-Leninist theory in general, the Marxist-Leninist economic doctrine in particular, from the attacks of the enemies of Leninism - Trotskyites, Bukharinites, bourgeois nationalists, and of particular importance for the fate of socialism in the USSR and throughout the world, the defense and further development of Lenin's teaching on the possibility of the victory of socialism in one country, Lenin's theory of the socialist revolution, had a defense.

In a number of Stalin's works ("On the Foundations of Leninism", "On the Questions of Leninism", "Economic Problems of Socialism in the USSR", reports at congresses and conferences of the CPSU), Lenin's theses are developed on the economic and political essence of imperialism and the general crisis of capitalism, on the patterns of development of the monopoly capitalism. Relying on Lenin's classical instructions about the economic essence of imperialism, which consists in the domination of monopolies, about monopoly high profits, Stalin formulated the basic economic law of modern capitalism. He gave a detailed analysis of the general crisis of capitalism and its two stages: the first, which began during the First World War, and the second, which unfolded during the Second World War, especially after the people's democracies in Europe and Asia fell away from the capitalist system.

Exposing the servants of the bourgeoisie, who sing of the capitalist system of economy, he proved that modern capitalism is in a state of general all-round crisis, embracing both the economy and politics. The most striking expression of the general crisis of capitalism is the world-historic victory of the Great October Socialist Revolution in the USSR and the split of the world into two systems - capitalist and socialist. An integral part of the general crisis of capitalism is the crisis of the colonial system of imperialism.

Stalin's works elucidate the essence and significance of such features of the general crisis of capitalism as the extreme aggravation of the market problem, the chronic underutilization of enterprises, and constant mass unemployment. Having given an analysis of the changes in the nature of the capitalist cycle and economic crises in the modern era, Stalin showed the futility of the attempts of the bourgeois state to fight crises, the groundlessness of assertions about the possibility of a planned economy under capitalism. Stalin's writings exposed the deeply reactionary and aggressive essence of fascism and the treacherous role of contemporary right-wing socialists.

Marxist-Leninist political economy, as well as the theory of Marxism-Leninism as a whole, finds its further development and enrichment in the decisions of the Communist Party of the Soviet Union and the fraternal communist parties, in the works of Lenin's disciples - the leading figures of the Communist Party of the Soviet Union, the leading figures of the fraternal communist parties.

[1] K. Marx, Capital, vol. I, 1953, p. 12.

[2] K. Marx, Capital, vol. I, 1953, p. 13.

[3] V. I. Lenin, Three sources and three components of Marxism, Works, vol. 19, p. 7.

[4] V. I. Lenin, Three sources and three components of Marxism, Works, vol. 19, p. 3.

[5] V. I. Lenin, Historical fate of the teachings of Karl Marx, Works, vol. 18, p. 546.

NOTES

(1) Lenin, Imperialism, the Highest Stage of Capitalism

(2) Lenin, Introduction to "N.I. Bukharin: Imperialism and World Economy"

(3) N.I. Bukharin, Imperialism and World Economy

(4) Lenin, Address To The Second All-Russia Congress Of Communist Organisations Of The Peoples of The East

(5) Lenin, Lecture on the Proletariat, and War

(6) Lenin, The Social-Chauvinists' Sophisms

(7) Lenin, Junius Pamphlet

(8) Lenin, Extraordinary Seventh Congress of the R.C.P.(B.)

(9) Lenin, Report On Foreign Policy

(10) Lenin, Left-wing Communism

(11) Stalin, Report on the Work of the Central Committee to the Eighteenth Congress of the C.P.S.U.(B.)

(12) Lenin, Under a False Flag

(13) Lenin, Speech At A Meeting In Butyrsky District

(14) Stalin, Economic Problems of the USSR, 1951

(15) Stalin, 7th Extended Plenary Session of the ICCI

(16) Stalin, Notes on modern topics

(17) Stalin, On the results of the July Plenum of the Central Committee of the All-Union Communist Party of Bolsheviks